"This isn't just a book of Sister Pie's best recipes, it's a testament to what happens when you build a business that has more than one bottom line. This is a book about a community and about how sustaining community can be so sweet (. . . and savory)."

—JULIA TURSHEN, author of *Now & Again*, *Feed the Resistance*, and *Small Victories*

"I've yet to find a more lovely place in Detroit than this kitchen full of women making pies. We're all so lucky that Lisa has distilled her baking magic into a book that we can bake (and dance) our way through at home."

—JOY THE BAKER, author of *Joy the Baker Over Easy*

sister pie

sister pie

The Recipes & Stories of a Big-Hearted Bakery in Detroit

Lisa Ludwinski

PHOTOGRAPHS
E.E. Berger

LORENA JONES BOOKS
An imprint of TEN SPEED PRESS
California | New York

This book is dedicated to the people of Sister Pie:
our staff, customers, neighbors, farmers, and friends.

CONTENTS

AND EVERYTHING ELSE

PROLOGUE

I'm Lisa Louise Ludwinski, the owner of Sister Pie and the author of this book. I wrote this manuscript over the course of one year, sending out recipes to testers each month and camping out at my computer whenever I wasn't at the bakery. As it turns out, I'm at the bakery *a lot*. I struggled and stressed to find time. Even when I could pull myself away, I couldn't shift gears. My creativity and focus were at an all-time low. "How's the cookbook going?" would throw me into a dual state of panic and denial. I'd either stammer complete gibberish in reply or launch into a spoken novel, almost certainly leaving the inquirer wishing they'd kept quiet. I began to resent the project and cursed myself for not waiting five more years, by which time things would almost certainly have settled down. (Don't quote me on that.) Finally, I decided to do the unthinkable: take one month off. I knew that if I could physically remove myself from the daily operations of the bakery, I could make my deadline. Thankfully, the fourteen other women who run Sister Pie were up for the task of covering the day to day without me.

I'm grateful for this opportunity to capture and preserve the spirit of our young, wide-eyed pie shop, reflect on our beginnings and experience, and share the joy, terror, and confidence I've found through repetition and improvisation in the kitchen. I've written these recipes in the hope that they will inspire you, through the whimsy and heart conveyed on the pages, to run into your kitchen and bake pie (and more) for the people you love. Make this book a familiar friend—if you're anything like me, the pages will become stained with cherry juice, made sticky from spilled maple syrup, and be dog-eared, creased, and doodled on.

OUR SISTORY, SO FAR
(COMPLETE WITH DANCING)

I wasn't born an entrepreneur or a business owner or even a boss. Actually, scratch that. I am admittedly bossy to my core. A Lucy van Pelt type, my family might say. But in the past, that bossiness always translated to performance: dancing, acting, directing, and even miming. Yeah, I mimed. Let's (not) talk about it later.

As a young lass growing up in small-town Milford, Michigan, home of the General Motors Proving Grounds, I had three ambitions: to be a baker, a hair cutter, and a movie star. Given the natural advantages I was born into, they all seemed well within my toddler self's reach. I soon gained a sister and we grew up together making home videos, going to Catholic school, playing with three dogs, watching *Ready . . . Set . . . Cook*, camping in our parents' motor home, and stealing chocolate chips from the pantry as often as possible.

Eventually I pursued my theatre passions at a tiny liberal arts college in Kalamazoo, Michigan. (Go Hornets!) From there I moved to the great big city of New York, with plans to open my own all-female theatre company, through which I'd have the creative license to act in and direct challenging, nontraditional plays. But first I needed a job or two. I worked part-time nannying two wonderfully sweet children, and part-time serving lattes to the stroller set, all while considering how I could break into directing.

I got distracted by food. My train ride reads were focused on learning about the ethics of food from Michael Pollan and the practical application of those ethics from Barbara Kingsolver. I spent my free time staring at recipes from blogs and newspapers with insatiable curiosity and joined the member-owned, member-worked Park Slope Food Co-op.

I began filming a low-budget, goofy cooking show called *Funny Side Up* on my MacBook set atop the refrigerator in my various Brooklyn apartments. The tagline was "Lisa makes herself food. Lisa makes yourself laugh." I approached it with tenacity, not blinking once to consider whether I looked foolish. After a hundred episodes, both successes and failures, I retired the ol' *Funny Side Up* show. I had started working behind the counter at Momofuku Milk Bar, a bakery owned by Christina Tosi, whom I deeply admired for her playfulness and pluck. I begged to get behind-the-scenes experience, and before I could say "corn cookie" I was baking my heart out in their Williamsburg commissary. I considered this my test: would my love of baking fade in the transition from home to professional? Negative. I felt exhilarated by the challenge of baking on a large scale and learning something new nearly every day. Staff enrichment came naturally: I led group stretches each morning and co-organized the first annual Milk Bar Holiday Sweets Swap. Gripped with the excitement of a developing skill, I began to consider what I could start on my own. I spent a summer moonlighting at another women-run business, Four & Twenty Blackbirds, making and rolling out pie dough for glorious hours on end. This new dream, coupled with a growing ache to return to Michigan, precipitated a major change in the way I saw my life going.

PIE FOR THANKSGIVING, AND FROM "I" TO "WE"

According to my early-development notes, I wanted to open a good-food, do-good kind of place that emphasized the importance of happy employees and sustainable food-business practices. A first-time trip to San Francisco left me feeling energized by places like Bi-Rite Market and Arizmendi Bakery. Anytime I'd visit my home state, a strong magnet would pull me to Avalon International Breads in Detroit and any of the Zingerman's community of businesses in Ann Arbor.

After six years in New York, I moved back to Milford and launched my business from my parents' kitchen for the Thanksgiving holiday, selling and baking forty pies for family and friends. I continued the baking marathon from Milford that December, but I was anxious to get to Detroit and dedicated the following year to planning my next move.

I signed up for a business class through an organization called Build: Institute, and joined a community of like-minded food entrepreneurs called FoodLab, honing my business plan and connecting with my peers and soon-to-be neighbors, respectively. In the meantime, I continued to live with my parents, develop new recipes, and crank out pie for my small but dedicated customer base. It's important to say here how profoundly grateful I am for my mother and father's support during Sister Pie's first year (and beyond). Not many entrepreneurs have the chance to focus nearly 100 percent of their time on business development, and the fact that I could made an incredible impact.

Why Sister Pie? The name is inspired by a term of endearment that my younger sister, Sarah, and I share for each other. As in, "What's shakin', Sister Pie?" The name triggered a concept, inspired by the image of women gathered around a kitchen counter, pitting cherries, rolling out pie dough, and talking with one another.

Why pie? Pie was the thing that could simultaneously showcase Michigan's abundance of farms and local produce (Michigan is second only to California in agricultural diversity) and fulfill my burgeoning desire to foster family-style community in the workplace. Pie, by its nature, inspires generosity—fundamentally, it's meant to be shared. Plus, it's pie. Everyone loves pie.

Sister Pie, which at that point was still just me and my rolling pin, celebrated one year in business by moving into a shared commercial kitchen space on Woodward Avenue, right in the heart of midtown Detroit. Even better, Sister Pie gained one eager intern, Anji, who brought with her an extra set of hands, a dedicated hustle, and a passionate spirit. As part of her initiation, she sliced apples for hours on end to contribute to our 150-pie production that Thanksgiving. We were growing!

THE PRE-PIE SHOP YEARS

The growth continued: Our newly acquired commercial license allowed us to establish wholesale accounts across town, we fundraised through the Kiva Detroit crowdfunding platform so we could afford to officially hire Anji as a part-time employee, and our eyes remained peeled for a permanent location. David from Parker Street Market, one our first wholesale accounts, would text me just hours after we delivered a tub full of pies to say they had sold out. As a result, I ended up traveling back and forth constantly from midtown to West Village. It felt like both a good omen and a clear sign, not only of positive neighborhood reception but that people would travel to get to Sister Pie. In the early summer of 2014, we set our eyes on a shop at the corner of Parker and Kercheval. We rented the space and began to host "Future Sister Pie Work Days," inviting family and friends to help demolish walls and tear up floors—paid in cookies, of course. It was invigorating and exhausting.

We spent 2014 and some of 2015 working toward opening the damn bakery as fast as we could. We calculated that opening would eventually cost us over $200,000, taking into account not only the cost of equipment and build-out but also three months of payroll, ingredients, and paper goods to prepare us for the unknown. And I had moved back from New York with only a security deposit to my name. Seeking funding, we entered the Hatch Detroit contest, an opportunity for start-up businesses in the city of Detroit to win a $50,000 grant. Newfound friends Maddie, Mike, and Emilia donated their time and passion to meeting our thriving demand, as we were still running a business. After making it to the top ten contestants, Anji and I ran around for two weeks straight trying to garner votes from the community and online networks. I wore my Sister Pie T-shirt every day (thanks, Dad!) and talked with anyone I encountered about the contest, from grocery cashiers to bartenders. For better or for worse, I had no shame. Turns out that it was for the better. We won!

After that victory, I buzzed around meeting with the architect/designer, fixing up the budget, shopping for furniture and supplies, applying for nontraditional loans, supervising the build-out, and, of course, continuing to bake pies.

#DANCEBREAK

The dancing started in the springtime of our second year. I cannot tell you how many times I'd stop what I was doing to break out into dance. The stress release turned me into a grinning, twirling loon. Eventually Anji started filming these dance breaks for Instagram posts and couldn't help but join in step. We had a two-woman show on our hands and gained a surprisingly (confoundingly) large audience. Song choices ranged from Boyz II Men and the Ramones to Genesis and Mariah Carey. Sometimes they told a story, other times they were silly for silly's sake.

Still hurting for funds toward the end of the build-out, we decided to throw a 24-hour dance party at a West Village record shop called Paramita Sound. We launched an Indiegogo campaign with the goal of raising $25,000, the contribution perks varying from a dozen buckwheat cookies to a design-a-pie experience. Anyone who gave money got a ticket to the dance party, at which I danced for the full 24 hours straight. Local businesses chipped in with sponsorships of food and drinks. Guest DJs from around the city and neighborhood (including a couple of elementary schoolers—shout out to Henry and Stella!) spun tunes. We ended up with upwards of $26,000 and more than a few bruised toes.

Sister Pie the bakery opened on a bright corner in Detroit's West Village on the east side of town on April 24, 2015, with a line out the door and a dozen new employees, and we've been hustling and dancing ever since.

THE MISSION AND CULTURE OF SISTER PIE

Each day, we feed a broad audience of neighbors, commuters, out-of-towners, and friends. The menu is nontraditional in flavor combinations, rustic in execution, and constantly changing to honor the local agriculture of Michigan. We strive to test the limits of our creativity while challenging and pleasing the palates of Sister Pie enthusiasts. We make our pie dough by hand daily and, most often, communally. We're a light-hearted bunch with a big-hearted mission: to serve food, our neighborhood, and each other.

Our mission statement reads: *"Sister Pie celebrates the seasons of Michigan through pie, cookies, breakfast, and lunch. Together we are a triple-bottom-line business, working to support our employees, our environment, and our economy. Together we provide consistently delicious, thoughtful, and inventive food. Together we foster a welcoming, friendly atmosphere for employees and customers through transparency, accessibility, community engagement, and education."*

What does that look like in practice? It's a work in progress (and heck, the mission statement itself is a work in progress), but we'll proudly share where we're at right now. Decisions become easier when we can ask ourselves if we're honoring the content of that statement.

EMPLOYEES ONLY

CAFE Loveless MOTEL

EAT. ♡
SLEEP. ♡
MAKE PIE. ♡
HAVE A COOKIE. ♡
DRINK PLENTY OF WATER. ♡
HUSTLE. ♡
TAKE A LITTLE #DANCEBREAK. ♡
CLEAN, CLEAN, CLEAN. ♡
ENJOY YOUR WORK. ♡
SUPPORT YOUR TEAM. ♡
BE KIND.

Sister Pie celebrates the seasons of Michigan through pie, cookies, breakfast, and lunch.

You'll read the word *seasonal* more than a couple times throughout this book. We work with farmers who grow food and flowers within 500 miles of Detroit, and our pie flavors change in sync with the harvest. That means no apple pie in May and no cherry pie in November. This commitment gives us our much-needed structure for creativity and enables us to work in harmony with the growers and nature. The produce tastes better. We appreciate it more.

Together we are a triple-bottom-line business, working to support our employees, our environment, and our economy.

I first heard of the triple-bottom-line (TBL) concept while doing a weeklong internship at Avalon International Breads in Detroit and subsequently learned how to apply it when I became a member of FoodLab Detroit. Traditionally, businesses work with one bottom line: their profit. A triple bottom line redefines the profit component and adds people and the planet to the equation. To recap, a commitment to people plus planet plus profit equals success. Or, as we say in our mission statement, "our employees, our environment, and our economy."

The TBL is an accounting strategy that can be tough to measure. Right now, our focus is on sustainability and establishing what it means for us. We pay our employees above-average wages, promote from within, and offer clear and communicative training plans. We recycle, implement monthly water-usage goals, and buy compostable paper goods from a local supplier. Our neighbor collects our eggshells and coffee grounds for his community garden. The Sister Pie-It-Forward program allows our customers to pre-purchase pie slices for anyone to use for any reason. Whether it's for someone who is short on change or someone who has never tried our pie before, this supports our mission of accessibility. We build and proudly share a vision for our business while developing strategic plans to get there. We pay our taxes. Future goals include health benefits, paid off-site training for further development, significant reduction of plastic use, and an annual internal audit that is unique to us and measures our growth.

Together we provide consistently delicious, thoughtful, and inventive food.

This one's easy. We want our food to taste good, and to be accessible and nourishing to the people we serve. We want to use our imagination, and to create flavors that are unique but not domineering.

Together we foster a welcoming, friendly atmosphere for employees and customers through transparency, accessibility, community engagement, and education.

We set out to create a people-first business. Our business doesn't survive or have purpose without people, whether it's our employees, our customers, or our neighbors. We teach pie-making classes, offer neighborhood discounts, value customer service, and run a monthly meeting for the businesses in the area. The Sister Pie Townhall meeting that we hold for our employees is by far my favorite example.

One Monday night a month, our staff gathers at our big communal table to share conversation over a meal. It's voluntary, and we're thrilled at how many people show up each time to have an open discussion about how we're running the business. The managers share financial reports, sales goals, office projects, and growth plans before we turn the floor over to the team. Both the emptying of a suggestion box and an open forum initiates an honest practice of communication and action.

There is so much to gain from these meetings. They get us to slow down and notice what's happening around us. Our

initial idea of what was right for the business and community might change depending on what we hear. Listening is hard, and patience harder still.

At the intersection of Parker and Kercheval, our home within the historic West Village neighborhood, there's a small, paved park-like plaza across the street where kids set up lemonade stands and customers picnic with pie on tree-wrapped benches built by neighbors. On our stretch of block alone is a barber shop, a gym, a day care, a real estate office, a florist, a wine bar, a French café, a hair salon, a gallery, and a bicycle store. But our neighborhood is primarily residential, which means we happily feed a stream of regular customers. Walking home to my apartment after a day at the shop, I'll run into Leon and his family, or Molly and hers. They live right next to Sister Pie, and have welcomed us since day one. I'll pass Vittoria, who runs the Hatch Contest, and we'll chat about what's next for Sister Pie. There's an email group for communicating events, crime, and missing or found pets. The neighborhood association hosts an annual summer picnic. The warmth of the neighborhood extends beyond its historic boundaries, reaching far south to Jefferson Avenue on the river, north to Mack Avenue, and to Islandview to our west and Indian Village to our east.

West Village is down the street from Belle Isle, the city's greatest park. My dear friend Meagan works for the Parks Department, and would gleefully chat with you about each and every park in the city. While starting a business can often feel like a lonely endeavor, you are certainly not alone in Detroit. There is a friend to make at every turn, so long as you say hello.

I've met more than my fair share of unique and interesting food entrepreneurs with do-good missions, and have been honored to partner with them for pop-ups, wholesale relationships, or just good, long chats. I'm proud to introduce you to a few of them here—people who have inspired me. The city of Detroit is rich with food, music, and art, so I asked them to share their favorites.

I love eating at New Center Eatery in the New Center area. They have the best waffles in the world, and the best part is it's a small business that has survived the crisis of Detroit and they're still here!

> —April Anderson, owner of Good Cakes and Bakes

My favorite thing to do here is take an early evening swim at Belle Isle Beach. There is nothing better after a long day than letting it all melt away with good friends, a solid swim, and the sunset over the Detroit city skyline.

> —Alexandra Clark, owner of Bon Bon Bon

Early in the morning or sometimes when the sun is so bright it's shining off the water, the Riverwalk leading to the crazy, intense Joe Louis Arena steps is my favorite thing about Detroit. I like the peacefulness and stillness of the water, and, of course, depending on the time of day, the people-watching is good, too. I have spent many a hot summer day jogging down the Riverwalk to tackle those steep Joe Louis steps. It's our own Detroit gym! A place I find my stride and a little bit of peace.

> —Espy Thomas, co-owner of Sweet Potato Sensations

My favorite place to eat is Detroit Vegan Soul. The food is always delicious. The customer service is always top-notch, and I love supporting two Black women entrepreneurs.

> —Malik Yakini, executive director and co-founder of Detroit Black Community Food Security Network and D-Town Farms

If this book at all inspires you to visit our fair city, you'll be well equipped to enjoy it, thanks to these folks. Until then, let's make some pie.

SISTER PIE PRIMER

I've divided the book into two major sections: The Pie, followed by And Everything Else. This structure reflects our story as we grew from a home-baked pie business to a brick-and-mortar shop with a fully stocked pastry case and a staff of kind, unique, and hard-working women. Throughout, I've provided notes on details I think might be helpful to you, whether it's how to approach recipes from start to finish or the ingredients to stock your shelves with as you bake and cook through this book.

For everything pie related, you'll reference The Pie (page 19). That half of the book contains what you need to know about making pie dough, rolling out crust, mixing up fillings, whipping up meringues, and baking the final product. Begin by reading through The Dough and The Crust, then bookmark each. You'll flip back and forth between these chapters and the seasonal pie chapters. When you're not in a pie mood (as if!), you'll reference And Everything Else (page 143) to find recipes for cookies, bars, sweet and savory breakfast items, and even salad.

STEPS TO RECIPE SUCCESS

Here you'll find a list of best practices when it comes to baking from this book, all directly discovered through the kitchen mistakes I've made over the years.

Read a recipe from start to finish, maybe even twice, including any pages that have been listed for related ingredients or steps. From there, you can make a game plan, beginning by asking yourself these questions: *What do I need to get from the grocery store or market? Is this a one-day process or a two-day process? If I don't have access to a particular ingredient, what could I substitute?* I've made sure to explain which steps need rests or chilling so that you can properly strategize.

Once you've read through the recipe, created your game plan, and gathered your ingredients, it's time to set up your *mise en place*, or what we refer to simply as our "mise." The phrase translates from French to "everything in its place," and it's an essential work step. (I nearly wrote "it's essential for beginners," but then I considered the times I've gotten distracted in the kitchen, forgotten whether I've added the salt, and had to start over. It's essential for beginners and distractable bakers like me.)

To properly set up your mise, measure all ingredients separately as they are listed in the recipe. If a recipe calls for vegetables or fruit to be sliced (or diced), do that first. If a recipe calls for a cup of flour, measure that first. While most pastries require precise measurements for success, pies are much more forgiving. We've chosen to write the recipes in volume measurements (cups and spoons) instead of weight measurements (grams) with that in mind. When you go to measure dry ingredients, dip the measuring cup in the container and use a butter knife to level it. If a recipe calls for "1 tablespoon ground pistachios," it means that the pistachios should be ground, not whole, when you measure them. Once you've traveled down the list, you are ready to begin the recipe.

BAKING WITH THE BEST OF 'EM
Know your oven. We worked with at least nine different home ovens throughout the process of recipe testing for this cookbook, and we learned early on that each one has a mind of its own. Here are two recommendations for becoming better friends with yours:

1   Invest in an oven thermometer; most grocery stores sell them for under ten dollars, and you can see how your actual oven temperature corresponds to what it says on the dial.

2   Do a hot-spot test: Pour a cup of sugar onto a parchment-lined baking sheet and evenly spread it around. Transfer the baking sheet to a 400°F oven for 10 minutes. Remove the baking sheet from the oven and notice where the sugar has started melt— those are the hottest spots in your oven.

If the sugar is evenly affected throughout, you don't need to worry about rotating your baking sheets throughout the baking process. If it is fairly uneven, take note and plan accordingly.

If you are baking cookies or hand pies, you will need more than one baking sheet. Feel free to place two sheets in the oven at once, but keep in mind that you might need to add more time to the recipe and rotate the sheets from top to bottom during baking.

When we are training pastry cooks on the ovens at Sister Pie, we give baking times but emphasize that they are merely suggestions. You know your oven better than I do, which means I can't guarantee that what works in my oven will work exactly the same in yours. More important is paying attention to the visual cues. What does the recipe say it should look like or feel like? Before you know it, you'll even develop an internal baker's clock and beat the timer to the punch.

KITCHEN WISDOM
Patience is to baking as Daryl Hall is to John Oates: absolutely essential. Pay close attention to a recipe's timing. Our world is turning into a get-what-you-want-when-you-want-it place, but baking requires some old-fashioned waiting around. While you could hurry through pretty much any recipe and still create something edible, the experience will be easier and the final product happier if you've followed it exactly as written. I'm frustrated when I see pie dough recipes that instruct you to rest your pie dough for a measly thirty minutes before rolling out. If you give it the full rest it needs, which is two hours according to us, you won't be out of touch, but you'll probably be a little out of time. Worth it.

SISTER STAPLES: INGREDIENTS WE LOVE

Our flavor combinations are inspired by our passion for ingredients. We're especially keen on using nuts, seeds, fresh herbs, citrus, alternative flours, edible flowers, and cheese. Here is a list of those ingredients—our favorites to work with in the bakery—complete with advice to help make sure you're buying the right things. If a recipe in this book calls for an uncommon ingredient (as many of them do), I've included it in at least one other recipe. I know you don't want a pantry filled with special ingredients and no plan for using them!

Apple cider vinegar: This tangy all-purpose vinegar is used in our All-Butter Pie Dough and a majority of our salad dressings. See page 22 for more on why we love it.

Buckwheat flour: I first used buckwheat to make our signature chocolate chip cookies (page 163) but have since found so many other ways to use this naturally gluten-free flour. It has an intensely earthy flavor, especially as it ages, and is great as the sole flour in brownies and cookies. For lighter uses, we like to pair it with all-purpose flour at a 25:75 ratio. We buy a locally grown and milled buckwheat flour from Hampshire Farms but also recommend the easily found Arrowhead Mills brand.

Buckwheat groats: Before there is flour, there are groats. We buy bags of these protein-packed seeds to use for salads, porridge, and granola. Did I mention that buckwheat is related to the rhubarb plant?

Butter: Plugrá is our European-style baking butter of choice. See page 22 for more on why we love it.

Coconut, a love story: We use a total of five different forms of coconut throughout this book. It's one of those rare ingredients that

can be used as a replacement for both dairy and flour, in addition to being a textural superhero of deliciousness. Here are the varieties you'll find in our recipes:

Coconut milk: We use full-fat coconut milk from a can. Make sure to stir it up thoroughly after opening, as the fat will have risen to the top while the can sat on the shelf.

Coconut oil: We use an unrefined, virgin coconut oil that does not impart a ton of flavor. However, many unrefined coconut oils *do* give off a strong coconut flavor, so you could opt for the refined version instead.

Coconut flakes: We buy large, unsweetened, chip-like coconut flakes from Bob's Red Mill.

Shredded, unsweetened coconut: These tiny flakes, also from Bob's Red Mill, can serve as a partial flour replacement in recipes.

Shredded, sweetened coconut: Perhaps the most familiar coconut from a bag, these flakes are long, chewy, and sweet. We prefer using bags from Trader Joe's, as their version does not contain anything other than coconut meat, sugar, and salt. Or look for another natural product with the same qualities.

Cream cheese: Sometimes you can't stray from the classic, especially when it comes to cream cheese. We're avid Philadelphia brand lovers and use it pretty much anywhere we can. Not only does it act as the perfect shield at the bottom of a pie shell, but it adds just the right note of acidity and creaminess to muffin centers and bun fillings.

Dairy: Good dairy is the secret to so many of our Sister Pie staples. We've sourced most of our dairy products from Guernsey Dairy in Northville, Michigan, since we opened and love their thick, full-flavored milk and cream for pies, scones, and our daily batch of whipped cream pie topping. Find the equivalent of Guernsey Dairy wherever you live.

Dried beans: We buy organic dried beans from a local farmer and use them in two different ways at the shop. For blind-baking pies (see page 50), we use 1½ pounds of dried beans per pie, typically pinto and black beans, to hold the sides of the crust in place while it bakes. For salads and hand pies, we'll soak dried beans overnight in lots of water, then cook them on the stove in a big pot of water for about 2 hours, or until tender.

Edible flowers: You'll find recipes containing edible flowers of all kinds throughout the book. We use edible dried rose petals and lavender buds, in addition to a couple other dried flower products. Most tea and spice stores sell these ingredients, and online merchants also have them.

Egg wash: Our standard egg wash is just that: whole eggs, beaten together until homogeneous and uniformly yellow in color.

Fine yellow cornmeal: Soft, light, and unmistakably corny, the stone-ground cornmeal from our local mill is one of our obsessions. It's in every chapter, multiple times. If you can find freshly ground cornmeal at your farmers' market, all the better. If not, we prefer Arrowhead Mills Organic Yellow Cornmeal.

Flaky sea salt: We're big on salty-sweet flavor profiles, and the large flakes do just the trick for a clean, strong finish. We buy Maldon Sea Salt by the bucket but also recommend Jacobsen Salt Co.

Fresh herbs: You'll find a variety of verdant fresh herbs called for throughout this book. They bring a brightness to sweet and savory recipes that completely changes the game.

Maple syrup: The majority of the maple syrup we buy ends up in our fan-favorite Salted Maple Pie, but we also turn to it to sweeten up our granola, scones, and various salad dressings. Look for a good-quality Grade B variety, which has a darker and more intense flavor than Grade A.

Nuts and seeds: These tiny powerhouses of fat and flavor are added to many of our recipes to provide textural diversity. Recipes will specify whether you should buy them salted or not.

Pistachios: I simply cannot get enough pistachio in my life. These green nuts are rich with flavor and work insanely well in sweet applications. I add them to almost anything (cookies, salads, granola, pie), and you should too. All recipes in this book call for shelled roasted and salted pistachios.

Poppy seeds: These nutty little seeds make me think of salad dressing and bagels, and I'm quite simply obsessed. Beautiful with a pop of crunch, they can take a recipe from ho-hum to holy mackerel.

Spelt flour: Within the realm of alternative flours, spelt is one of our favorites. Its mildly sweet and nutty flavor makes it an excellent substitute for white or whole wheat flours. We particularly love it in muffins and scones for a new spin on old favorites.

Sugar-Sugar: This Sister Pie original ingredient is an equal-parts mix of turbinado and granulated sugars. Start by making a batch containing 1 cup of each—you'll use it over and over again as you bake through this book.

Sweet potatoes: Farmer Norm brings us sweet potatoes throughout the year, and we love them for more than just their hearty nutritional value. Their natural ability to go sweet or savory or both makes them extremely versatile. Buy the kind with bright orange skins, and be sure to wash them well—we almost never peel them.

Tahini: This Middle Eastern staple made simply of ground sesame seeds offers a distinctive nutty, toasty element to dishes. We prefer Soom brand tahini (run by three sisters!), for its well-rounded flavor and silky smooth texture.

Tapioca starch: I tried potato starch, cornstarch, arrowroot, and tapioca when testing the early Sister Pie fruit filling recipes. Tapioca starch, often referred to as tapioca "flour," mixed with fruit yields fillings that set when cooled but doesn't impart any flavor or gel consistency.

Turbinado sugar: Often labeled "raw" or "Demerara," turbinado is used in many of our recipes as a substitute for granulated white sugar, or as part of a mix. It imparts a subtle toffee flavor.

Valrhona cocoa powder: Like butter, cocoa powders come in a wide range of choices, but they can be worlds apart in flavor. We choose Dutch-process Valrhona for its deep chocolate taste.

Vanilla extract: Even though you're typically only using a few teaspoons in a recipe, a good-quality, pure vanilla extract makes all the difference when it comes to the flavor of your final product. We default to Nielsen Massey brand, specifically the Madagascar Bourbon variety, which is readily available in most major grocery stores.

Whole spices: We love toasting whole spices before adding them to baked goods and salads. By using the whole spice, you get a much fresher and more potent flavor than with its ground counterparts. Plus, the aroma you're left with post-toasting is heaven on earth.

GLOSSARY OF TOOLS WE REFER TO WHEN WE TALK ABOUT DOING STUFF

Throughout the book, you might encounter some new kitchen lingo if you're not regularly running around with bench scrapers and pastry blenders, as we are. Here is a list of our favorite tools. You can find most of these at Webstaurant.com or other online vendors, but may we respectfully recommend supporting your local, independent cookware supplier?

Bench scraper: This is hands down my favorite kitchen tool and a mainstay on our kitchen bench. In terms of versatility, it is a queen. And you're a queen, too, so you need queen-like tools. You can blissfully portion dough, clean off countertops, scoop up vegetables, cut up sticks of butter, and more.

Disher scoops: We use a variety of different-sized disher scoops to portion out cookies at the bakery to ensure that they all come out the same size. Their uses extend far beyond the realm of cookie baking, and we use them for tasks like filling muffin tins, making meatballs, and, obviously, scooping ice cream. The numbers (like 24, 40) and colors (yellow, purple) designate the size (the higher the number, the smaller the scoop) and are standard across the board. The recipes indicate the number and color of scoop to use, as well as alternative ways of measuring portions.

Offset spatula: The 9½-inch offset spatula is my second favorite tool (after the aforementioned bench scraper). Its small size and sleek shape makes it perfect for spreading a filling on the bottom of a pie shell, smoothing a brownie or bar batter, or swirling a meringue top.

Pastry blender: A reliable pastry blender is vital to creating pie dough, scones, and crumble toppings. Be sure to find one with a sturdy handle and sharp blades for maximum efficiency.

Peeler: When it comes to personal peeling preferences, I tend to be partial to the Y-peeler versus the common swivel peeler. Either will work great in these recipes, but I've just found that I have a bit more control with the Y variety. I also appreciate the ability to easily peel from the top to the bottom of an item, especially when working through a hefty prep list.

Pastry wheel: This is basically the smaller cousin of the tool you'd traditionally use to slice up a pizza. We find them particularly helpful in cutting out pie dough rounds and trimming strips of lattice with the greatest of ease. Use the side with the straight edge if the pastry wheel you purchased has two blades.

Pie pans: We like baking with metal pie tins—not only are they excellent conductors of heat, they also allow us to safely use our preferred blind-bake method (page 50) without fear of breakage. We use recyclable aluminum tins at the shop that are 9 inches wide and 1³⁄₁₆ inches deep. If you've got only glass or ceramic pie plates, you can still make wonderful pie, but skip the freezer step for all recipes. Not working with a 9-inch tin? We've made sure that our roll-out instructions leave a little room for flexibility.

Sheet pans: Arm yourself with a good set of sheet pans and you can do anything, like sledding down a snowy hill . . . or baking lots of our Sister Pie cookies. Use standard aluminum half-sheet pans (18 by 26 inches), and remember to load up on parchment paper so that your treats don't stick to the pans. In recipes, we'll always refer to these as "baking sheets."

Spice grinder (for spices only): Sometimes our recipes call for a small amount of a ground ingredient, such as spices, nuts, and dried flowers. Instead of lugging out the food processor for such jobs, we default to our dedicated spice grinder for quick blitzes. It's simply a coffee bean grinder that we use only for baking purposes. It's fast, it's easy, and there's minimal cleanup afterwards.

Stainless steel bowls: Stainless is my material of choice when it comes to mixing bowls. Not only does it hold up to pastry blender and bench scraper beatings without breaking or scratching, but it also retains cold temperatures well. This is especially handy when it comes to keeping all of your butter chunks cold during pie dough and scone prep.

Tapered rolling pin: The tapered style of rolling pin is a classic tool in traditional European baking. Unlike handled rolling pins, where you hold on to the handles that extend from the ends and roll back and forth, the tapered rolling pin allows you to gently apply pressure to specific portions of the dough while rolling it. This enhanced control helps create an evenly thick dough and makes it much easier to maintain your pie crust's circular shape.

THE ART OF KITCHEN IMPROV

When I was in college, my Wednesday and Sunday nights were strictly dedicated to rehearsals for our school's improv team, Monkapult. We'd prance around playing games and crafting long, elaborate story sequences. Improv granted me the invaluable skill of being bold enough to work with what I have. I'm better equipped as a baker (and as a boss . . . and gosh darn it, as a human being!) to take every opportunity to make something new or better.

When the shop opened, I was always the first one to arrive and the last one to leave. I'd do a little bit of everything, from setting out the pastry display to making staff lunch to counting out the nightly deposit. The best part, by far, was the daily improvisation. Due to the fast-paced, ever-changing nature of the Michigan growing season, that first summer we baked whatever kind of pie with whatever kind of fruit and made no apologies. We experimented with flours, cheeses, and seeds in the dough and went to town with decorative crimps, lattices, and steam-vent designs. Eventually, business owner demands and cookbook writing took over, and while they, too, are creative endeavors, I've been anxious to get back to the kitchen and play.

I encourage you to follow suit and goof around with your baking and cooking, but remember that within creativity, structure is key. Trying to act in an improv scene without a prompt or style—a blank slate—is cruel and unusual punishment (and also just bad theatre). It's the same in the kitchen. Once you master a recipe, you should have the confidence to strut around the pantry, adding this and that.

THE PIE

I'm convinced that anyone who says they don't like pie hasn't tasted a good crust. Honestly, what's not to like? It's flaky, buttery sheets of pastry enveloping tart, juicy fruit with just the right amount of sugar and spice and a little bit of fresh whip on top. Okay, not all pie is like that. But we're here to help, so read closely and remember this: All good pie starts with good pie dough. Treat pie dough with the same respect that you would fleeting sour cherries, and you'll be off to a great start. As I say to the students at our pie dough classes: Intention, action. Since we want to work quickly to avoid butter meltdown, I've aimed to be clear about the "what" and the "why" of the directions you'll read here. This will help you build that dough instinct and learn when you've gone too far (or not far enough).

The keys to mastery are easy enough—repetition and patience—if you're game for practicing. It's only through spending an afternoon in your kitchen with a couple pounds of butter, making this recipe over and over again, that you'll begin to develop the necessary intuition for crust-making success. From there, the possibilities are truly endless; we add seeds, cheese, alternative flours, herbs, and more to our standard recipe. This chapter walks you through the steps of making our classic All-Butter Pie Dough as well as a number of variations found in the recipes throughout this book. But first, the basics.

When making pie: You'll notice that there aren't specific dough or roll-out instructions in each recipe, but instead we refer to the relevant pages from The Dough (page 21) and The Crust (page 43). You can structure your approach to a recipe however you like, but I find it most helpful to have my dough made, rolled out, and blind-baked (when applicable) before starting on a filling.

The importance of a butter splurge: If you can track down a block of European-style Plugrá butter, you're well on your way to winning the blue ribbon at the county fair. The first time I tried pastries made with Plugrá, I swore I'd never go back. What makes it so special is a high butterfat percentage and low water content, ensuring a powerfully flavorful and flaky crust. At our pie dough classes, we begin the lesson with a butter taste test. Give it a try and find out for yourself.

All cold everything: The secret to the best crust is not only the full-fat flavor of the butter but its temperature. Once it is out of the fridge, if butter begins to warm up too much, it will start to melt and become homogeneous with the rest of the ingredients when blended. For pie crust, you want those cold, pea-size butter bits to retain their structure in the mixed dough and to burst when the crust hits the hot oven, creating the flakiest pockets imaginable. If you happen to have especially warm hands, place your mixing bowl and pastry blender in the fridge or freezer for about 15 minutes before you make the dough.

Icy water, now improved and with tang: While working at Brooklyn's Four & Twenty Blackbirds for a summer, I learned a number of good tricks that considerably changed my pie dough–making experience. Here's one of my favorites: Fill a 1-cup liquid measuring cup with about 1 inch of water and freeze until completely frozen. Just after you mix your dry ingredients, grab it from the freezer and fill with water plus 2 tablespoons or so of apple cider vinegar. The ice-cold water-vinegar mixture should look just like apple juice. Let it chill on your counter while you mix the other ingredients for the dough.

The addition of vinegar to pie dough was originally thought to tenderize the gluten (thus avoiding a tough crust), but there isn't any good scientific evidence proving that it makes a difference. We keep it in our recipe for its tangy flavor and our respect for tradition.

Not the pie-baking plan-ahead type? That's okay! When you're ready to make the dough, simply fill a 1-cup liquid measuring cup about halfway with ice, then add water and 2 tablespoons apple cider vinegar.

Turn, baby, turn: Rotating the bowl during the pie dough–making process and rotating the dough during the rolling-out process helps achieve a consistent, even dough.

You versus your food processor: We make our pie dough in batches approximately four times the size of the ones in this book. No machines are used at any step in the process. Not only is it hard to find a gadget that could hold the amount of butter we use, but we believe that our dough just tastes better because it's made by humans with lots of love. However, there's no shame in pulling out your food processor to quickly mix up a batch of pie dough, crumble, or streusel. The important part to remember, when it comes to this method, is that the pulse button is your friend and the process button is your enemy. Pulsing emulates the traditional hand-cutting method and helps keep those precious butter chunks intact. First add your dry ingredient mixture to the bowl of the food processor and pulse two or three times to blend. Add your cold butter chunks and pulse eight to ten times, until the butter chunks are roughly the size of peas. Slowly add your cold liquid through the feed tube while pulsing to bring the dough together. For streusels and crumbles, simply transfer the mixture to an airtight container and chill. For pie dough, dump the dough onto a lightly floured surface and lightly knead it together with your fingertips before shaping and wrapping.

Gettin' fancy with alternative crusts: Once you've mastered the All-Butter (AB) Pie Dough, it'll be time to graduate to alternative doughs. While AB is straightforward and simple, like pop music, these doughs add nuance and depth to your pies. And really, you can do whatever the heck you want with a variety of alternative flours, ground nuts, grated cheese, herbs, flowers, and spices.

The method for making alternative pie doughs is exactly the same as for the AB recipe. Just incorporate enough of the additions to recognize the flavor, but not so much that you mess with the handleability and flake factor of the dough. If you're adding cheese, cut it in with the pastry blender as soon as you've reached the peas and Parmesan stage, and just moments before adding the ice water.

Any dry additions (ground nuts, for example) can be added to the flour at the beginning of mixing.

Just store it: After making the dough, you should wrap it tightly in plastic wrap, twice. The first wrap is to keep out any air or moisture, while the second wrap ensures that last night's leftovers don't infiltrate your pure butter flavor. It can stay wrapped in your fridge for a few days (and up to a week is probably just fine), or in the freezer for about a year. If frozen, transfer the dough to the fridge one full day before rolling out.

Throw a pie party: Can I come? Seriously, baking multiple pies for an event or Thanksgiving is no joke. Since I started Sister Pie out of a home kitchen, I know a thing or two about baking in bulk. Don't be afraid to scale up—our pie dough recipe easily multiplies by four. You're gonna need a big bowl, but that'll come in handy for scaling up filling recipes as well. Go through the recipes and note which steps can be made in advance, because the best way to successfully bake a lot of pies at a time is to start two or three days early. Ideally, all you're doing on the last day is assembling, baking, and finishing.

Okay, we've laid the foundation. Now get to work!

This is our go-to dough, and it's how each pie begins. Every pie baker, professional or at home, seems to have an opinion on the best combination of fats for the flakiest crust—is it lard, shortening, butter, or a mix? Our basic dough is a pure and simple ode to unsalted butter and all-purpose flour—we think it produces the best-tasting, lightest, flakiest pie crust. ♥

ALL-BUTTER PIE DOUGH

Makes 2 discs, enough for one 9-inch double-crust lattice-topped or full-top pie or two 9-inch single-crust pies

2½ cups all-purpose flour

1 teaspoon granulated sugar

1 teaspoon kosher salt

1 cup (2 sticks) unsalted European-style butter, straight from the fridge

½ cup ice-cold water-vinegar mixture (see page 22), or more if needed

In a large stainless steel bowl, combine the flour, sugar, and salt and stir to mix well. Place the sticks of butter in the bowl and coat on all sides with the flour mixture. Using a bench scraper, cut the butter into ½-inch cubes. Work quickly to separate the cubes with your hands until they are all lightly coated in flour. Grab that bench scraper once again and cut each cube in half. I always tell my pie dough students that it's unnecessary to actually cut each cube perfectly in half, but it's a good idea to break up the butter enough so that you can be super-efficient when it's pastry blender time.

It's pastry blender time! Switch to the pastry blender and begin to cut in the butter with one hand while turning the bowl with the other. It's important not to aim for the same spot at the bottom of the bowl with each stroke of the pastry blender, but to actually slice through butter every time to maximize efficiency. When the pastry blender clogs up, carefully clean it out with your fingers (watch out, it bites!) or a butter knife and use your hands to toss the ingredients a bit. Continue to blend and turn until the largest pieces are the size and shape of peas and the rest of the mixture feels and looks freakishly similar to canned Parmesan cheese.

At this point, add the water-vinegar mixture all at once, and switch back to the bench scraper. Scrape as much of the mixture as you can from one side of the bowl to the other, until you can't see visible pools of liquid anymore. Now it's hand time. Scoop up as much of the mixture as you can, and use the tips of your fingers (and a whole lot of pressure) to press it back down onto the rest of the ingredients. Rotate the bowl a quarter-turn and repeat. Scoop, press, and turn. With each fold, your intention is to be quickly forming the mixture into one cohesive mass. Remember

CONTINUED

to incorporate any dry, floury bits that have congregated at the bottom of the bowl, and once those are completely gone and the dough is formed, it's time to stop.

Remove the dough from the bowl, place it on a lightly floured counter, and use your bench scraper to divide it into two equal pieces. Gently pat each into a 2-inch-thick disc, working quickly to seal any broken edges before wrapping them tightly in a double layer of plastic wrap. If you're portioning for a lattice-topped pie, shape one half into a 2-inch-thick disc and the other half into a 6 by 3-inch rectangle. Refrigerate the dough for at least 2 hours or, ideally, overnight. When you go to roll out the crust, you want the discs to feel as hard and cold as the butter did when you removed it from the fridge to make the dough. This will make the roll-out way easier.

You can keep the pie dough in the fridge for a few days or in the freezer for up to 1 year. If frozen, remove the dough and place it in the refrigerator to thaw one full day before you intend to use it. If you're planning to make only one single-crust pie, wrap the discs separately and place one in the freezer.

We use this dough for all of our savory hand pies. ♥

ALL-BUTTER HAND PIE DOUGH

Makes enough for 10 hand pies

3¾ cups all-purpose flour

1½ teaspoons granulated sugar

1½ teaspoons kosher salt

1½ cups (3 sticks) unsalted European-style butter, straight from the fridge

¾ cup ice-cold water-vinegar mixture (see page 22), or more if needed

In a large stainless steel bowl, combine the flour, sugar, and salt and stir to mix well. Place the sticks of butter in the bowl and coat on all sides with the flour mixture. Using a bench scraper, cut the butter into ½-inch cubes. Work quickly to separate the cubes with your hands until they are all lightly coated in flour. Grab that bench scraper once again and cut each cube in half. I always tell my pie dough students that it's unnecessary to actually cut each cube perfectly in half, but it's a good idea to break up the butter enough so that you can be super-efficient when it's pastry blender time.

It's pastry blender time! Switch to the pastry blender and begin to cut in the butter with one hand while turning the bowl with the other. It's important not to aim for the same spot at the bottom of the bowl with each stroke of the pastry blender, but to actually slice through butter every time to maximize efficiency. When the pastry blender clogs up, carefully clean it out with your fingers (watch out, it bites!) or a butter knife and use your hands to toss the ingredients a bit. Continue to blend and turn until the largest pieces are the size and shape of peas and the rest of the mixture feels and looks freakishly similar to canned Parmesan cheese.

At this point, add the water-vinegar mixture all at once, and switch back to the bench scraper. Scrape as much of the mixture as you can from one side of the bowl to the other, until you can't see visible pools of liquid anymore. Now it's hand time. Scoop up as much of the mixture as you can, and use the tips of your fingers (and a whole lot of pressure) to press it back down onto the rest of the ingredients. Rotate the bowl a quarter-turn and repeat. Scoop, press, and turn. With each fold, your intention is to be quickly forming the mixture into one cohesive mass. Remember to incorporate any dry, floury bits that have congregated at the bottom of the bowl, and once those are completely gone and the dough is formed, it's time to stop.

CONTINUED

Remove the dough from the bowl, place it on a lightly floured counter, and use your bench scraper to divide it into two equal pieces. Gently pat each into a 1-inch-thick square, working quickly to seal any broken edges before wrapping them tightly in a double layer of plastic wrap. Refrigerate the dough for at least 2 hours or, ideally, overnight. When you go to roll out the crust, you want the squares to feel as hard and cold as the butter did when you removed it from the fridge to make the dough. This will make the roll-out way easier.

You can keep the hand pie dough in the fridge for a few days or in the freezer for up to 1 year. If frozen, remove the dough and place it in the refrigerator to thaw one full day before you intend to use it.

This small-batch, textural superstar dough should serve as the foundation for the many summer galettes in your baking future. You can substitute whole wheat or spelt flour for the cornmeal, and lavender buds or jasmine for the rose petals. It appears here in this book as the basis for the Apricot Raspberry Rose Galette (page 64). ♥

CORNMEAL ROSE GALETTE DOUGH

Makes enough for one 7-inch galette

¾ cup all-purpose flour

3 tablespoons fine yellow cornmeal

1½ tablespoons dried, edible rose petals

½ teaspoon granulated sugar

½ teaspoon kosher salt

6 tablespoons (¾ stick) unsalted European-style butter, straight from the fridge

3 tablespoons ice-cold water-vinegar mixture (see page 22), or more as needed

In a large stainless steel bowl, combine the flour, cornmeal, rose petals, sugar, and salt and stir to mix well. Place the block of butter in the bowl and coat on all sides with the flour mixture. Using a bench scraper, cut the butter into ½-inch cubes. Work quickly to separate the cubes with your hands until they are all lightly coated in flour. Grab that bench scraper once again and cut each cube in half. I always tell my pie dough students that it's unnecessary to actually cut each cube perfectly in half, but it's a good idea to break up the butter enough so that you can be super-efficient when it's pastry blender time.

It's pastry blender time! Switch to the pastry blender and begin to cut in the butter with one hand while turning the bowl with the other. It's important not to aim for the same spot at the bottom of the bowl with each stroke of the pastry blender, but to actually slice through butter every time to maximize efficiency. When the pastry blender clogs up, carefully clean it out with your fingers (watch out, it bites!) or a butter knife and use your hands to toss the ingredients a bit. Continue to blend and turn until the largest pieces are the size and shape of peas and the rest of it feels and looks freakishly similar to canned Parmesan cheese.

At this point, add the water-vinegar mixture all at once, and switch back to the bench scraper. Scrape as much of the mixture as you can from one side of the bowl to the other, until you can't see visible pools of liquid anymore. Now it's hand time. Scoop up as much of the mixture as you can, and use the tips of your fingers (and a whole lot of pressure) to press it back down onto the rest of the ingredients. Rotate the bowl a quarter-turn and repeat. Scoop, press, and turn. With each fold, your intention is to be quickly forming the mixture into one cohesive mass. Remember to incorporate any dry, floury bits that have congregated at the bottom of the bowl, and once those are completely gone and the dough is formed, it's time to stop.

Remove the dough from the bowl, place it on a lightly floured counter, and gently pat it into a 1-inch-thick disc, working quickly to seal any broken edges before wrapping it tightly in a double layer of plastic wrap. Refrigerate the dough for at least 2 hours or, ideally, overnight. When you go to roll out the crust, you want the disc to feel as hard and cold as the butter did when you removed it from the fridge to make the dough. This will make the roll-out way easier.

You can keep the galette dough in the fridge for a few days or in the freezer for up to 1 year. If frozen, remove the dough and place it in the refrigerator to thaw one full day before you intend to use it.

The fall day when the first wheel of two-year aged Gouda rolls into the shop is an occasion for dancing. It's got that magical crystallized texture in some bites, and a buttery, creamy smoothness in others. We use this for our Apple Sage Gouda Pie (page 89), but you could also use it to make savory galettes or hand pies. ♥

AGED GOUDA PIE DOUGH

Makes enough for one 9-inch lattice-topped pie

2½ cups all-purpose flour

1 teaspoon granulated sugar

1 teaspoon kosher salt

1 cup (2 sticks) unsalted European-style butter, straight from the fridge

1 ounce aged Gouda, grated

½ cup ice-cold water-vinegar mixture (see page 22), or more if needed

In a large stainless steel bowl, combine the flour, sugar, and salt and stir to mix well. Place the sticks of butter in the bowl and coat on all sides with flour. Using a bench scraper, cut the butter into ½-inch cubes. Work quickly to separate the cubes with your hands until they are all lightly coated in the flour mixture. Grab that bench scraper once again and cut each cube in half. I always tell my pie dough students that it's unnecessary to actually cut each cube perfectly in half, but it's a good idea to break up the butter enough so that you can be super-efficient when it's pastry blender time.

It's pastry blender time! Switch to the pastry blender and begin to cut in the butter with one hand while turning the bowl with the other. It's important not to aim for the same spot at the bottom of the bowl with each stroke of the pastry blender, but to actually slice through butter every time to maximize efficiency. When the pastry blender clogs up, carefully clean it out with your fingers (watch out, it bites!) or a butter knife and use your hands to toss the ingredients a bit. Continue to blend and turn until the largest pieces are the size and shape of peas and the rest of it feels and looks freakishly similar to canned Parmesan cheese. Speaking of cheese, now is the time to add the Gouda and mix it in quickly with the pastry blender until it is evenly distributed.

At this point, add the water-vinegar mixture all at once, and switch back to the bench scraper. Scrape as much of the mixture as you can from one side of the bowl to the other, until you can't see visible pools of liquid anymore. Now it's hand time. Scoop up as much of the mixture as you can, and use the tips of your fingers (and a whole lot of pressure) to press it back down onto the rest of the ingredients. Rotate the bowl a quarter-turn and repeat. Scoop, press, and turn. With each fold, your intention is to be quickly forming the mixture into one cohesive mass. Remember to incorporate any dry, floury bits that have congregated at the bottom of the bowl, and once those are completely gone and the dough is formed, it's time to stop.

Remove the dough from the bowl, place it on a lightly floured counter, and use your bench scraper to divide it into two equal pieces. Gently pat one into a 2-inch-thick disc, working quickly to seal any broken edges before wrapping it tightly in a double layer of plastic wrap. Pat the other half into a 6 by 3-inch rectangle. Refrigerate the dough for at least 2 hours or, ideally, overnight. When you go to roll out the crust, you want the disc to feel as hard and cold as the butter did when you removed it from the fridge to make the dough. This will make the roll-out way easier.

You can keep the pie dough in the fridge for a few days or in the freezer for up to 1 year. If frozen, remove the dough and place in the refrigerator to thaw one full day before you intend to use it.

One stupidly simple way to make a dynamic pie dough is to replace 20 to 25 percent of the flour with toasted nuts or seeds. We make our Brandy Pecan Pie (page 99) only in November and December, so we go all out with double pecan action. You could also use this dough to make Pie Sandwich Cookies (see page 159) with ganache filling. ♥

TOASTED PECAN PIE DOUGH

Makes enough for one single-crust 9-inch pie

1 cup all-purpose flour

¼ cup ground toasted pecans (see opposite)

1 teaspoon kosher salt

1 teaspoon granulated sugar

½ cup (1 stick) unsalted European-style butter, straight from the fridge

¼ cup ice-cold water-vinegar mixture (see page 22), or more if needed

In a large stainless steel bowl, combine the flour, pecans, salt, and sugar and stir to mix well. Place the stick of butter in the bowl and coat on all sides with flour. Using a bench scraper, cut the butter into ½-inch cubes. Work quickly to separate the cubes with your hands until they are all lightly coated in flour. Grab that bench scraper once again and cut each cube in half. I always tell my pie dough students that it's unnecessary to actually cut each cube perfectly in half, but it's a good idea to break up the butter enough so that you can be super-efficient when it's pastry blender time.

It's pastry blender time! Switch to the pastry blender and begin to cut in the butter with one hand while turning the bowl with the other. It's important not to aim for the same spot at the bottom of the bowl with each stroke of the pastry blender, but to actually slice through butter every time to maximize efficiency. When the pastry blender clogs up, carefully clean it out with your fingers (watch out, it bites!) or a butter knife and use your hands to toss the ingredients a bit. Continue to blend and turn until the largest pieces are the size and shape of peas and the rest of it feels and looks freakishly similar to canned Parmesan cheese.

At this point, add the water-vinegar mixture all at once, and switch back to the bench scraper. Scrape as much of the mixture as you can from one side of the bowl to the other, until you can't see visible pools of liquid anymore. Now it's hand time. Scoop up as much of the mixture as you can, and use the tips of your fingers (and a whole lot of pressure) to press it back down onto the rest of the ingredients. Rotate the bowl a quarter-turn and repeat. Scoop, press, and turn. With each fold, your intention is to be quickly forming the mixture into one cohesive mass. Remember to incorporate any dry, floury bits that have congregated at the bottom of the bowl, and once those are completely gone and the dough is formed, it's time to stop.

Remove the dough from the bowl, place it on a lightly floured counter, and gently pat it into a 2-inch-thick disc, working quickly to seal any broken edges before wrapping it tightly in a double layer of plastic wrap. Refrigerate the dough for at least 2 hours or, ideally, overnight. When you go to roll out the crust, you want the disc to feel as hard and cold as the butter did when you removed it from the fridge to make the dough. This will make the roll-out way easier.

You can keep the pie dough in the fridge for a few days or in the freezer for up to 1 year. If frozen, remove the dough and place it in the refrigerator to thaw one full day before you intend to use it.

TOAST IT UP

Many recipes in this book call for toasted nuts, seeds, coconut flakes, or grains. You can toast most of these by adding them to a dry skillet over medium heat or placing them on a baking sheet in a preheated 350°F oven. The ingredients should lightly brown and smell up the joint with their nutty-seedy fragrance. If a recipe calls for toasted chopped or ground nuts, you will toast them before chopping or grinding.

This speckled, cheesy dough is what we use to make our classic Apple Cheddar Rye Hand Pies (page 139) every October and November. You could also use this dough to make savory crackers. Roll it out ¼ inch thick and use a pastry wheel to cut a grid of ½-inch squares. Reroll the scraps once. Transfer the squares to a parchment-lined baking sheet and brush with a beaten egg. Top with a few flakes of sea salt and bake in a 450°F oven until deep golden brown. If the rye flour makes your dough feel particularly dry, add 1 or 2 extra tablespoons of the ice-cold water-vinegar mixture. ♥

CHEDDAR RYE HAND PIE DOUGH

Makes enough for 10 hand pies

3 cups all-purpose flour

¾ cup dark rye flour

1½ teaspoons granulated sugar

1½ teaspoons kosher salt

1½ cups (3 sticks) unsalted European-style butter, straight from the fridge

2 ounces aged Cheddar cheese, grated

¾ cup ice-cold water-vinegar mixture (see page 22), or more if needed

In a large stainless steel bowl, combine the all-purpose and rye flours, sugar, and salt and stir to mix well. Place the sticks of butter in the bowl and coat on all sides with the flour mixture. Using a bench scraper, cut the butter into ½-inch cubes. Work quickly to separate the cubes with your hands until they are all lightly coated in flour. Grab that bench scraper once again and cut each cube in half. I always tell my pie dough students that it's unnecessary to actually cut each cube perfectly in half, but it's a good idea to break up the butter enough so that you can be super-efficient when it's pastry blender time.

It's pastry blender time! Switch to the pastry blender and begin to cut in the butter with one hand while turning the bowl with the other. It's important not to aim for the same spot at the bottom of the bowl with each stroke of the pastry blender, but to actually slice through butter every time to maximize efficiency. When the pastry blender clogs up, carefully clean it out with your fingers (watch out, it bites!) or a butter knife and use your hands to toss the ingredients a bit. Continue to blend and turn until the largest pieces are the size and shape of peas, and the rest of it feels and looks freakishly similar to canned Parmesan cheese. Speaking of cheese, now is the time to add the Cheddar and mix it in quickly with the pastry blender until it is evenly distributed.

At this point, add the water-vinegar mixture all at once, and switch back to the bench scraper. Scrape as much of the mixture as you can from one side of the bowl to the other, until you can't see

CONTINUED

visible pools of liquid anymore. Now it's hand time. Scoop up as much of the mixture as you can, and use the tips of your fingers (and a whole lot of pressure) to press it back down onto the rest of the ingredients. Rotate the bowl a quarter-turn and repeat. Scoop, press, and turn. With each fold, your intention is to be quickly forming the mixture into one cohesive mass. Remember to incorporate any dry, floury bits that have congregated at the bottom of the bowl, and once those are completely gone and the dough is formed, it's time to stop.

Remove the dough from the bowl, place it on a lightly floured counter, and use your bench scraper to divide it into two equal pieces. Gently pat each into a 1-inch-thick square, working quickly to seal any broken edges before wrapping them tightly in a double layer of plastic wrap. Refrigerate the dough for at least 2 hours or, ideally, overnight. When you go to roll out the crust, you want the squares to feel as hard and cold as the butter did when you removed it from the fridge to make the dough. This will make the roll-out way easier.

You can keep the pie dough in the fridge for a few days or in the freezer for up to 1 year. If frozen, remove the dough and place in the refrigerator to thaw one full day before you intend to use it.

BUCKWHEAT FLOUR AND PRODUCT CONSISTENCY

Because buckwheat isn't as widely available as, say, all-purpose flour, we've encountered a bit of trouble with consistency. Currently, we're proud to use a locally grown and milled buckwheat flour from Hampshire Farms that makes for a deeply earthy and nutty galette dough and cookie dough (see page 163). One time, farmer Randy accidentally milled the flour on a coarser setting and the cookies baked differently, with a bigger spread and a chewier crumb. Not better, not worse. Just different. Instead of sending the flour back, we kept it and used every last grain, embracing the inconsistency. In grand conclusion, use whatever the heck kinda buckwheat flour you want! If you can't find a good and weird local buckwheat flour, we've had good luck with Arrowhead Mills brand.

It's good to have an extra-sturdy dough for handheld slices of galettes, and we love the earthy heft that buckwheat flour brings to the baking bench. This dough, which we use to make our Egg-on-Top Sweet Potato and Cheddar Galettes (page 223), uses buttermilk as the ice-cold liquid addition for a tender and flavorful crust. If you'd like to make a double-crust fruit pie with this dough, simply package it into two 9-inch discs (see page 23). ❤

BUTTERMILK BUCKWHEAT GALETTE DOUGH

Makes 1 square pack for galettes

2 cups all-purpose flour

½ cup buckwheat flour

1 teaspoon granulated sugar

1 teaspoon kosher salt

1 cup (2 sticks) unsalted European-style butter, straight from the fridge

½ cup ice-cold buttermilk

In a large stainless steel bowl, combine the all-purpose and buckwheat flours, sugar, and salt and stir to mix well. Place the sticks of butter in the bowl and coat on all sides with flour. Using a bench scraper, cut the butter into ½-inch cubes. Work quickly to separate the cubes with your hands until they are all lightly coated in flour. Grab that bench scraper once again and cut each cube in half. I always tell my pie dough students that it's unnecessary to actually cut each cube perfectly in half, but it's a good idea to break up the butter enough so that you can be super-efficient when it's pastry blender time.

It's pastry blender time! Switch to the pastry blender and begin to cut in the butter with one hand while turning the bowl with the other. It's important not to aim for the same spot at the bottom of the bowl with each stroke of the pastry blender, but to actually slice through butter every time to maximize efficiency. When the pastry blender clogs up, carefully clean it out with your fingers (watch out, it bites!) or a butter knife and use your hands to toss the ingredients a bit. Continue to blend and turn until the largest pieces are the size and shape of peas and the rest of it feels and looks freakishly similar to canned Parmesan cheese.

At this point, add the buttermilk all at once, and switch back to the bench scraper. Scrape as much of the mixture as you can from one side of the bowl to the other, until you can't see visible pools of liquid anymore. Now it's hand time. Scoop up as much of the mixture as you can, and use the tips of your fingers (and

CONTINUED

a whole lot of pressure) to press it back down onto the rest of the ingredients. Rotate the bowl a quarter-turn and repeat. Scoop, press, and turn. With each fold, your intention is to be quickly forming the mixture into one cohesive mass. Remember to incorporate any dry, floury bits that have congregated at the bottom of the bowl, and once those are completely gone and the dough is formed, it's time to stop.

Remove the dough from the bowl, place it on a lightly floured counter, and gently pat it into a 1-inch-thick square, working quickly to seal any broken edges before wrapping it tightly in a double layer of plastic wrap. Refrigerate the dough for at least 2 hours or, ideally, overnight. When you go to roll out the crust, you want the square to feel as hard and cold as the butter did when you removed it from the fridge to make the dough. This will make the roll-out way easier.

You can keep the galette dough in the fridge for a few days or in the freezer for up to 1 year. If frozen, remove the dough and place in the refrigerator to thaw one full day before you intend to use it.

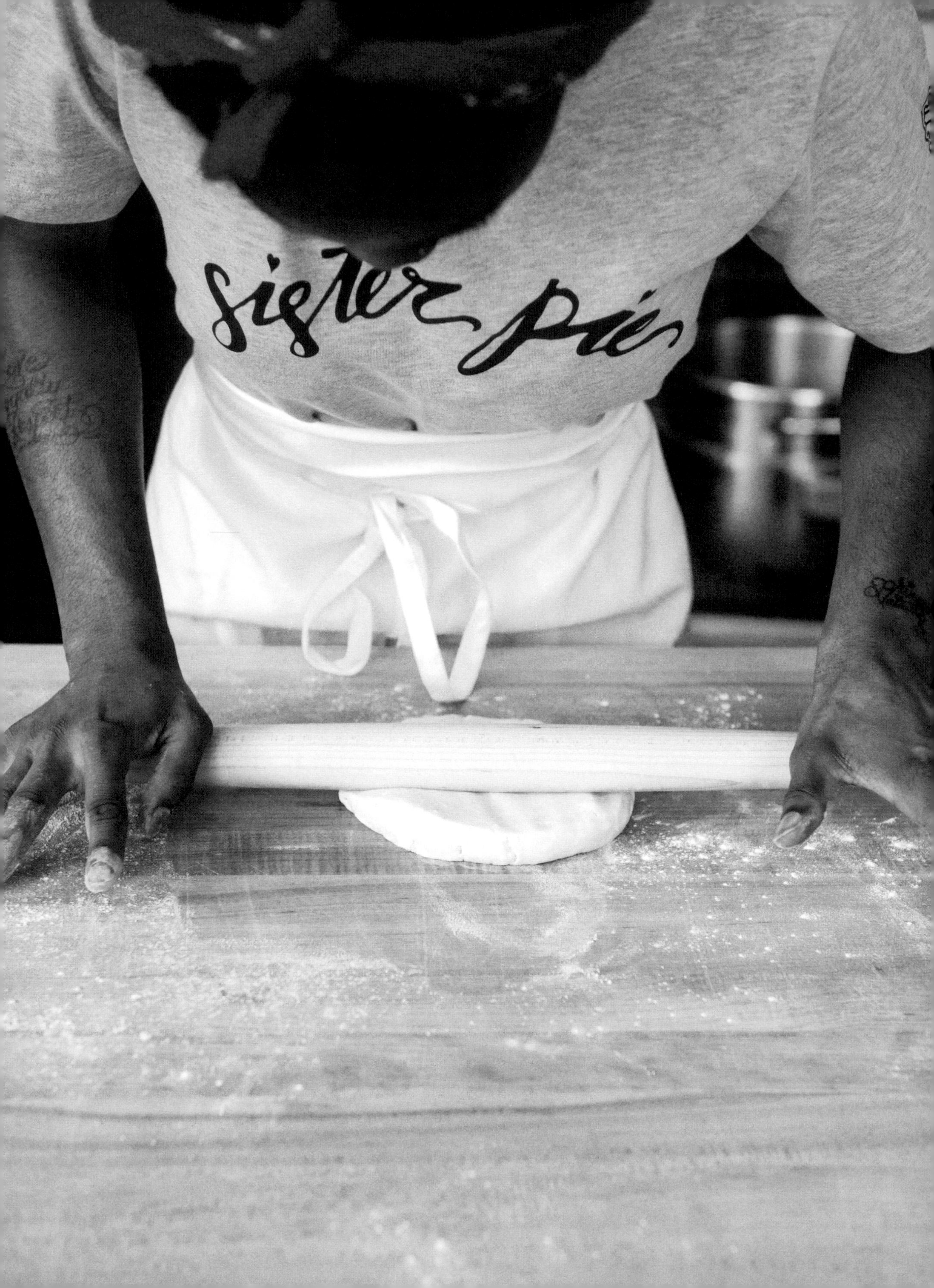
sister pie

the crust

While the students in our pie classes approach pie dough mixing with a healthy blend of fear and confidence, the terror really awakens when it's roll-out time. Rolling dough out to a circle of the proper size will come easy enough if you follow the instructions, but brace yourself for the crimps. You'll be developing, over time and with practice, a new skill in dexterity. I liken it to learning how to be a ceramicist (but that's just a guess). If you spend that idyllic afternoon in your kitchen making dough after dough, you can spend the next afternoon rolling them out. The first few tries might be rough, but rest assured that this is totally normal. Soon your newly developed natural instincts will kick in, and you'll have the best-looking pie in town. And if you don't, so what? A pie's aesthetic perfection never contributed anything to its taste.

We have a variety of roll-out styles for our pie dough, depending on whether we're making 9-inch pies, hand pies, galettes, lattice weaves, or others. Here you'll find instructions for rolling out every single one. When you bake from the recipes in this book, reference this section whenever it is time to roll out your pie dough.

A GUIDE TO ROLL-OUTS

There are three steps to a successful pie crust roll-out: The first step is pounding the dough to flatten it a bit and to bring its temperature up slightly. This helps improve roll-out efficiency, as it's easier to roll out a crust when it is thinner and the dough is more pliable. The second step is beginning to roll out the perimeter of the crust. By focusing on this early in the game, we lessen our chances of over-rolling the very edge of the dough. The third step is rolling out from the center until the dough reaches the desired size. We'll spend the most time on this step. With each step, the dough circle should increase in size by ½ inch to 1 inch at a time.

WHAT YOU NEED

1 disc dough for a 9-inch pie, straight from the fridge

Extra flour, for dusting

Rolling pin (we prefer the French tapered style)

9-inch metal or aluminum pie pan (see page 15),
lightly greased with softened butter

Pastry cutter or knife

THE 9-INCH ROLL-OUT

To roll out pie crust, lightly flour your work surface and place the unwrapped pie dough in the center. Using a rolling pin, begin by banging the dough from the left to the right, striking the dough about four times. Rotate the dough 180 degrees and bang across the dough from left to right once more.

Use one tapered end of the rolling pin to press and roll along the edge of the round one single time, enlarging the circle. After each press of the edge, rotate the disc 45 degrees clockwise. If you sense that the dough is sticking to the surface, lift it up and lightly flour the surface below it.

To begin the final step, place the rolling pin in the very center of the dough. Apply pressure to the pin while rolling it away from yourself (stand on your tiptoes to get maximum leverage if necessary), being careful to stop rolling about 1 inch away from the edge (to avoid over-rolling the areas you've already rolled). Rotate the disc 45 degrees and roll again. If it becomes difficult to rotate the dough, lift it up and lightly flour the surface beneath it. If the top surface of the dough starts to feel sticky, flip it over onto the floured counter and roll on the other side. Continue this

If you're rolling out the
top of a double-crust pie,
follow the instructions
given here, but cut the
top circle into a 10-inch
round. If you're rolling
out for the Apricot
Raspberry Rose Galette
(page 64), follow these
instructions but trim the
final circle into a 11-inch
round.

roll and rotation process until you have a circle 12 to 13 inches in
diameter. Gently run your rolling pin over the entirety of the dough
to make sure the final size is an even thickness.

Invert your pie tin or dish onto the circle. Using a pastry cutter
or knife, and the pie tin as a guide, cut a circle around the tin that
is 2½ to 3 inches larger than the edge of the tin. Gather up the
dough scraps, wrap in plastic wrap, and store in the fridge to
be added to other scraps and rerolled for another use. Remove
the pie tin and turn it right side up on the work surface. Fold the
dough circle in half. Place the folded dough in the pie tin so that it
covers one-half of the pan. Unfold the other half, and gently press
the dough to fit it snugly into the tin, making sure it is completely
centered and pressed all the way into the bottom of the tin.

What kind of pie are you making? If you're making a lattice-topped
or double-crust pie, put the pie tin in the fridge while you roll out
the rest of the dough and prepare the filling. Otherwise, move on
to crimping (page 49) and blind baking (page 50).

THE SAVORY HAND PIE ROLL-OUT

Before new pastry cooks at Sister Pie begin training on 9-inch dough roll-outs and crimping, they learn how to roll out hand pie dough. It's beginner-friendly and forgiving. You can reroll the scraps from hand pie dough once, along with any other chilled scraps you've accumulated. If you reroll too many times, however, the dough will begin to spring back, making for uneven circles.

WHAT YOU NEED
1 block All-Butter Hand Pie Dough (page 27), straight from the fridge
Extra flour, for dusting
Baking sheet
Rolling pin (we prefer the French tapered style)
4-inch round cutter

Line a baking sheet with parchment paper. Lightly flour your work surface and place the unwrapped pie dough in the center. Using a rolling pin, bang the dough from the left to the right, flattening the dough into a big square. Place the rolling pin in the very center of the dough and apply pressure to the pin while rolling it away from yourself (stand on your tiptoes to get maximum leverage if necessary), from the center to the far edge. Rotate the square and roll again. Flour the surface and flip the dough as needed to prevent sticking. Repeat this process until you have a big square of even thickness, about 16 inches across. Cut out hand pie rounds using a 4-inch round cookie cutter (for savory hand pies). Transfer to the parchment-lined baking sheet. Gather up the dough scraps, reroll, and add to the baking sheet. Wrap the baking sheet in plastic wrap, and refrigerate until you're ready to assemble the hand pies.

For sweet hand pies: Follow the instructions for rolling out hand pie dough, but cut each round using a 3-inch cutter.

For 6-inch galettes: Follow the hand pie roll-out instructions, but use a 6-inch circular cutter of some kind (we flip one of our small metal bowls upside down). Transfer to a baking sheet, wrap in plastic wrap, and refrigerate until you're ready to assemble the galettes. Reroll the scraps once.

THE LATTICE ROLL-OUT

Even the most wonky-looking lattice weaves will impress the pie lovers in your life. It's worth the effort and intimidation. The roll-out process is straightforward and much like rolling out hand pie dough (see opposite page). Have your ruler or measuring tape handy, and let's begin!

WHAT YOU NEED

One 6 by 3-inch rectangular block All-Butter Pie Dough (page 25), straight from the fridge

Extra flour, for dusting

Baking sheet

Rolling pin (we prefer the French tapered style)

Ruler

Pastry cutter or knife

Line a baking sheet with parchment paper. Lightly flour your work surface and place the unwrapped pie dough in the center. Using a rolling pin, bang the dough from the left to the right. Now roll out the dough to flatten it into a slightly larger rectangle. Fold up the rectangle in thirds, like a letter. Turn the dough over back onto the floured surface and repeat the banging from side to side. Place the rolling pin in the very center of the dough and apply pressure to the pin while rolling it away from yourself (stand on your tiptoes to get maximum leverage if necessary), from the center to the far edge. Rotate the square 180 degrees and roll again. Flour the surface and flip the dough as needed to prevent sticking. Repeat this process until you have a rectangle that is approximately 13 by 12 inches. Use a ruler and the pastry cutter to trim the very edges of the rectangle. Then, using the ruler as your guide, cut at least 6 strips of dough, each about 2 inches wide. Place the strips on the baking sheet, wrap in plastic, and transfer to the fridge until you're ready to assemble the pie. Gather up any dough scraps to be added to other scraps and rerolled for another use, wrap in plastic wrap, and refrigerate for up to 3 days.

GOT (EXTRA) LATTICE?

If you've happened to roll out more than 6 strips of lattice, or you've got scraps, here's an idea for using leftover strips: One of our pastry cooks, Tianna, had the brilliant thought to make something she calls Strawb' Sisters. Place any small piece of fruit (a strawberry, a peach slice, an apple wedge) on the end of one lattice strip, and roll it up entirely. Lay the roll on its side (looking at the cross-section view) in a small baking pan or on a parchment-lined baking sheet. Brush with egg wash, top with Sugar-Sugar (see page 12), and bake in a 450°F oven for 10 to 15 minutes.

CRIMP DRAMA

I like to call our crimps "dramatic" because nearly everyone at the pie class freaks out when they see just how much pressure I apply to the dough to achieve our distinctive decorative edge. No two crimps are created equal, making them a fun way to make your pie stand out from everyone else's.

To create a crimped edge for a single-crust blind-baked pie, roll the dough overhang toward the center of the pie, creating a ring of dough, as though you were rolling a poster tightly. I like to imagine that my thumbs are twiddling a little dance together. One thumb rolls over while the other thumb presses the dough down onto the tin's edge to seal. Right over left, right over left, or for lefties, left over right, left over right.

Use the thumb and index finger of one hand to form a "C," and position that hand in the very center of the pie pan. Position your opposite thumb on the outside of the pan. Use the "C" fingers to push and press the rim of the dough up and away from the pan, simultaneously pressing the thumb of your other hand into the "C" to make a crimp. Continue until the entire ring of dough is crimped. If you're right handed, you'll move clockwise; if you're left-handed, counterclockwise. At this point, put the crust in the freezer for at least 15 minutes. If you don't plan to use the crust that same day, wrap it tightly in plastic wrap and store it in the freezer for up to 1 year.

THE DOUBLE-CRUST OR LATTICE CRIMP

To assemble a pie with a top crust or lattice weave, you will follow the instructions for crimping almost exactly, but with the top crust or lattice in place. See pages 52–53 for a how-to on pie assembly.

THE WONDERFUL WORLD OF BLIND BAKING (FOR ALL SINGLE-CRUST PIES)

Approximately 80 percent of the pies we serve at Sister Pie begin with a blind-baked crust. We do it to ensure a flaky, well-done crust with every bite of pie. The art of blind baking is a funny, often finicky process that intimidated me for years. It took practicing over and over and over (during a newborn pie business's first Thanksgiving, no less) to finally achieve mastery. Here are some tricks I learned along the way.

Fully freezing our crusts before baking helps the crimps retain their shape and placement while achieving maximum flakiness. It's that whole cold-butter-bits-hitting-a-hot-oven thing we talked about earlier (see page 22). Skip the expensive pie weights (save your pennies for fancy butter) and load up on dried beans. You can use them again and again, and over time they develop a special aroma—all part of the charm of making lots of pie at home.

WHAT YOU NEED

One 9-inch crust, crimped and frozen for at least 15 minutes

Aluminum foil

1½ pounds dried beans (we use pinto and black, but use whatever you have)

Preheat your oven to 450°F with the rack on the lowest level. Remove the pie crust from the freezer, tear off a square of aluminum foil that is slightly larger than the pie shell, and gently fit it into the frozen crust. Fill the crust with the dried beans (they should come all the way up to the crimps) and place the pie pan on a baking sheet. Transfer the baking sheet to the oven and bake for 25 to 27 minutes. Check for doneness by peeling up a piece of foil—the crimps should be light golden brown. Remove the baking sheet from the oven and transfer to a cooling rack. After 6 minutes, carefully remove the foil and beans. You did it! You are now ready to fill the pie.

EXTRA BLIND BAKING

A few of the more sensitive pies in this book are baked at a lower temperature, which will protect the fillings from separating and curdling but will also result in a lighter crust. To make up for it, you'll start with an extra-blind-baked crust. Follow the instructions for blind baking up until you take it out of the oven. Immediately after removing the baking sheet from the oven, fold back the foil, exposing the crimps, but keep the bean package in the center of the tin. Brush the crimps with beaten egg and place the baking sheet back in the oven for another 5 to 7 minutes, or until the crust turns a deep golden brown.

LATTICE-TOPPED AND DOUBLE-CRUST PIES

While single-crust, blind-baked pies are more common at Sister Pie (and in this book), there's a special place for a pie with a top crust. To guarantee that the crust is well-done, these fully assembled pies start at the same high temperature we use for blind baking before dropping to a regular bake temperature of 350°F. Below I show you how to assemble these pies.

To weave a lattice, place one strip of lattice across the center of the filled pie. Take another strip and lay it on top, perpendicular to the first one, creating a cross. Lay the next two strips on either side of the first strip you laid down, so they are parallel to both each other and the original strip. Next, working with the original strip, fold back both ends toward the center, and then place the last two lattice strips down on either side of the second (perpendicular) strip. Fold the original strip back down, so that it lies across and on top of the newly placed strips. Does it look like a woven lattice yet? You're doing a great job!

To make a braided strip of lattice, cut one strip into 3 equal-width strips. Pinch them together at the top and then braid. Use in place of one wide strip.

Tear off the ends of the lattice pieces so they are flush with the perimeter of the pie tin. Roll the edge of the crust in, sealing the lattice. Crimp, using the technique described on page 49, being careful to push the crimps down and into the pie, as opposed to keeping them too loose on the edge.

STEAM VENTS

If you're making a double-crust pie without a lattice top, you'll want to cut vents before baking to allow steam to escape. (See page 102 for more.)

WHAT TO SERVE WITH PIE

We've been making fresh batches of whipped cream every day at Sister Pie since the beginning. Not only is it an ideal counterpart to pretty much any pie you can imagine, but it's also a perfect way to highlight our state's beloved Guernsey dairy. We use a basic ratio of 1 cup heavy whipping cream to 1 teaspoon granulated sugar and a pinch of salt, whisked together (either with a stand mixer, hand mixer, or metal whisk) until it reaches soft peaks. A dollop goes splendidly with the Salted Maple Pie (page 108), the Coffee Chess Pie (page 110), and the Malted Lime Pie (page 120), among many, many others.

You'd be hard pressed to find a more flawless pairing than pie and vanilla ice cream. We recommend going the à la mode route with fruit pies like the Sour Cherry Bourbon Pie (page 66) and Ginger Peach Biscuit Pie (page 75).

For a lighter topping option, we tend to default to thick plain yogurt. Its rich tartness works beautifully with earthy pie flavors like the Sweet Beet Pie (page 114), Cranberry Crumble Pie (page 91), and Rhubarb Rosemary Streusel Pie (page 58).

While we don't have any vegan pies in this book, this whipped coconut cream option is a good alternative for those trying to avoid dairy. Whipped coconut cream is made simply by mixing the thick, creamy top layer from a 14-ounce can of coconut milk (save the liquid to jazz up a smoothie or batch of soup) with about ¼ cup powdered sugar and a pinch of salt. As with the aforementioned whipped cream topping, use a stand mixer, hand mixer, or metal whisk and beat until you have soft peaks. We're quite partial to a bit of whipped coconut cream atop the Chocolate Coconut Pie (page 112) or the From Another Galaxy (Gluten-Free, Vegan) Brownies (page 178).

SPRING + SUMMER PIES

We're always in a bit of a hectic transition when spring hits at Sister Pie. All winter we've been cooped up working on bakery systems and making soup and then . . . boom. The first sunny day arrives and there's a line out the door. Visits to the market become a little less gray as tulips and rhubarb make their annual debut. We hustle through a host of pie holidays, from Mother's Day to Labor Day and everything in between. You'll find that this chapter of our year is jam-packed with herbaceous, floral flavors and a glorious amount of produce. It's a time of celebration. But first, a few tips for success.

Filling spilling: You'll notice that we call for all pies (and anything we bake, for that matter) to be on a parchment-lined, rimmed baking sheet. The fruit pies tend to bubble over onto the baking sheet—you'll almost always end up with a mess, but the parchment makes cleanup much easier.

That room-temp life: Anytime you make a nonfruit filling, the recipe will instruct you to have all of your ingredients at room temperature. I've noted this for refrigerated items, but you also need to pay close attention to warmed ingredients that should be cooled before being mixed in. Extreme contrasts in temperature among filling ingredients might result in seizing or crystallization.

Slice advice: Whip out your chef's knife to slice pies with ease. Dipping the knife in a pitcher filled with very hot water between slices helps create clean cuts, especially with meringue-topped pies. We'll often go over the slices with a small paring knife to make sure we've cut straight through to the bottom of the pan.

I'm a 100 percent rhubarb pie kinda person. I want it in every pie—in blueberry pie, strawberry pie, peach pie, and cherry pie. But the totally tart all-rhubarb filling is what gets me out of bed at the end of May. We buy 100 pounds of rhubarb at a time, lug it back to the bakery, and trim it all at once. Then we go about making this pie. The rosemary streusel adds a subtle perfume to the otherwise straightforward flavors in an homage to this superstar vegetable (yes, vegetable!) pie.

If the rhubarb stalks are wider than 1 inch, cut them in half lengthwise before slicing into 1-inch pieces. ♥

RHUBARB ROSEMARY STREUSEL PIE

Makes one 9-inch pie

ROSEMARY STREUSEL

¾ cup all-purpose flour

¼ cup whole wheat flour

½ cup packed light brown sugar

2 teaspoons finely minced fresh rosemary

¼ teaspoon kosher salt

½ cup (1 stick) unsalted butter, straight from the fridge

FILLING

1¾ pounds rhubarb, trimmed and sliced into 1-inch pieces (6 cups)

¾ cup granulated sugar

¼ cup turbinado sugar

¼ cup plus 2 tablespoons tapioca starch

⅛ teaspoon ground ginger

¼ teaspoon kosher salt

¼ teaspoon packed grated lemon zest

2 tablespoons cream cheese, at room temperature

Make the streusel: Combine the all-purpose and whole wheat flours, brown sugar, rosemary, and salt in a large metal bowl. Place the butter in the bowl and coat on all sides with the flour mixture. Take a bench scraper and cut the butter into ½-inch cubes directly into the flour mixture in the bowl. Work to break up the cubes with your hands until they are lightly coated with the flour mixture. Continue to use the bench scraper to cut the cubes into smaller pieces.

Switch to a pastry blender, and use a rocking motion to cut in the butter with one hand while turning the bowl with the other. It's important not to aim for the same spot at the bottom of the bowl with each movement, but to actually slice through butter every time. Once most of the butter is incorporated, use your fingers to fully break down the butter until the streusel resembles wet sand. Be careful not to overwork the mixture. The streusel can be made up to 2 days in advance and stored in the refrigerator.

When you're ready to assemble and bake the pie, preheat your oven to 350°F. Line a baking sheet with parchment paper.

Make the filling: In a large mixing bowl, toss the rhubarb with the granulated and turbinado sugars, tapioca starch, ginger, salt, and lemon zest. Toss with your hands until evenly distributed.

CONTINUED

One 9-inch crust made with All-Butter Pie Dough (page 25), blind baked and cooled (see page 50)

1 large egg, beaten

Using a small offset spatula or the back of a spoon, evenly spread the cream cheese on the bottom of the pie shell. Brush the crimped edge with the beaten egg. Layer the rhubarb on top of the cream cheese, being careful not to mound it in the center. Carefully cover the fruit with the streusel topping, leaving a small hole in the center of the pie to serve both as a steam vent for the fruit as it cooks and as an indicator of when the pie is done. If the hole closes up during baking, insert a knife to bust it back open. Place the assembled pie on the parchment-lined baking sheet.

Transfer the baking sheet with the pie on it to the oven and bake for 1½ to 2 hours, until the pie juices are beginning to bubble in the center and the streusel topping is a uniform deep golden color.

Remove the baking sheet from the oven and transfer the pie to a wire rack to cool for 4 to 6 hours. When the pie is at room temperature, slice it into 6 to 8 pieces and serve.

Store leftover pie, well wrapped in plastic wrap or under a pie dome, at room temperature for up to 2 days.

My dad, and maybe yours too, loves pistachios. He shells and eats them at what seems like a dangerous pace, between shouting out Jeopardy! answers before anyone else has a chance. This pie was created with him in mind, right in time for Father's Day, when the strawberries are at their June best.

This recipe calls for two pistachio preparations. For the crumble, use a chef's knife to chop them on a cutting board, ensuring a mix of fine and coarse nuts. For the topping, grind the pistachios in a spice grinder or food processor until they are the consistency of flour. ♥

STRAWBERRY PISTACHIO CRUMBLE PIE

Makes one 9-inch pie

PISTACHIO CRUMBLE

½ cup finely chopped toasted pistachios (see page 35)

½ cup rolled oats

½ cup all-purpose flour

⅓ cup packed light brown sugar

¼ teaspoon ground cardamom

½ teaspoon grated lime zest

¼ teaspoon kosher salt

½ cup (1 stick) unsalted butter, straight from the fridge

FILLING

¼ cup granulated sugar (add an extra 2 tablespoons if your strawberries aren't very sweet)

¼ teaspoon grated lime zest

1 tablespoon freshly squeezed lime juice

¼ cup plus 1 tablespoon tapioca starch

¼ teaspoon kosher salt

2 pounds whole strawberries, hulled (6½ cups)

Make the crumble: In a large mixing bowl, combine the pistachios, rolled oats, flour, brown sugar, cardamom, lime zest, and salt. Place the butter in the bowl and coat on all sides with the flour mixture. Take a bench scraper and cut the butter into ½-inch cubes directly into the flour mixture in the bowl. Work to break up the cubes with your hands until they are lightly coated with the flour mixture. Continue to use the bench scraper to cut the cubes into smaller pieces—the idea is that you are cutting each cube in half.

Switch to a pastry blender, and begin to cut in the butter with one hand while turning the bowl with the other. It's important not to aim for the same spot at the bottom of the bowl with each movement, but to actually slice through butter every time. You'll need to clean out the pastry blender every few turns of the bowl. Once most of the butter is incorporated, use your fingers to fully break down the butter until it is no longer visible and you're working with small clusters of crumble. Be careful not to overwork the mixture. The crumble can be made up to 2 days in advance and stored in the fridge.

When you're ready to assemble and bake the pie, preheat your oven to 350°F. Line a baking sheet with parchment paper.

CONTINUED

2 tablespoons cream cheese, at room temperature

One 9-inch crust made with All-Butter Pie Dough (page 25), blind baked and cooled (page 50)

1 large egg, beaten

2 tablespoons finely ground toasted pistachios (see page 35)

Make the filling: In a large bowl, combine the sugar, lime zest and juice, tapioca starch, and salt. Add the strawberries and toss with your hands until evenly distributed.

Using a small offset spatula or the back of a spoon, evenly spread the cream cheese on the bottom of the pie shell. Brush the crimped edge with the beaten egg. Layer the strawberries on top of the cream cheese, being careful not to mound them in the center. Carefully cover the fruit with the crumble topping, leaving a small hole in the center of the pie, to serve both as a steam vent for the fruit as it cooks and as an indicator of when the pie is done. If the hole closes up during baking, insert a knife to bust it open. Place the assembled pie on the parchment-lined baking sheet.

Transfer the baking sheet with the pie on it to the oven and bake for 1½ to 2 hours, until the pie juices are beginning to bubble in the very center and the crumble topping is uniformly a deep golden color.

Remove the baking sheet from the oven, transfer the pie to a wire rack, and cover with the pistachios. Let cool for 4 to 6 hours. When the pie is at room temperature, slice it into 6 to 8 pieces and serve.

Store leftover pie, well wrapped in plastic wrap or under a pie dome, at room temperature for up to 2 days.

STRAWBERRY PREP

To properly prepare strawberries for pie, you need to hull them. Hold a strawberry in your hand and use a paring knife to remove the stem, revealing the white center of the strawberry's top. Use the tip of the knife to carve a tiny hole at the top of the strawberry, then tip the knife to pop out the white flesh (aka the "hull"). If your strawberries are on the large side, quarter them. If they're on the small side, halve them. If they're tiny and raspberrylike, keep 'em whole.

It's hard to fill a pie with raspberries, and we're never really rolling in enough apricots to commit them to our regular pie menu. Thank goodness for the simple galette. It comes together in an actual flash and has a filling-to-crust ratio that can't be beat. This rendition stars the aforementioned fruits, with supporting roles played by cornmeal, rose petals (for a visually stunning, extra-texturally pleasing crust), and rose flower water (for a unique, delicate filling). ♥

APRICOT RASPBERRY ROSE GALETTE

Makes one 7-inch galette

FILLING

6 ounces apricots, sliced into ¼-inch pieces (1⅓ cups)

3 ounces raspberries (⅔ cup)

¼ teaspoon packed grated lemon zest

¼ teaspoon rose flower water

¼ cup turbinado sugar

⅛ teaspoon kosher salt

1 tablespoon tapioca starch

Cornmeal Rose Galette Dough (page 30), rolled out into an 11-inch circle and laid flat on a parchment-lined baking sheet and refrigerated

2 tablespoons cream cheese, at room temperature

1 large egg, beaten

1½ tablespoons Sugar-Sugar (page 12)

1 tablespoon dried, edible rose petals

Preheat your oven to 425°F.

Make the filling: Place the apricots and raspberries in a medium bowl, and combine with lemon zest and rose flower water. In a small bowl, combine the turbinado sugar, salt, and tapioca starch. Pour over the fruit and toss with your hands to distribute evenly.

Remove the baking sheet with the unbaked crust from the refrigerator. Using a small offset spatula or the back of a spoon, evenly spread the cream cheese on the center of the dough, leaving about a 1½-inch border. Carefully arrange the apricots and raspberries in a single layer on top of the cream cheese. Begin to seal the galette by folding up a 1½-inch-wide section where the cream cheese ends and pressing it down gently onto the filling. Fold up the piece directly next to it, and place it down at an angle, so that it covers the corner of the dough you just laid down. Continue to do this until the entire circle is complete.

Brush the top of the crust with the beaten egg, and sprinkle the Sugar-Sugar evenly over the crust and the filling. Place the baking sheet in the oven and bake for 25 minutes, or until the crust is golden brown. Reduce the oven temperature to 350°F and continue to bake for 1 hour, or until the fruit begins to bubble in the center.

Remove the baking sheet from the oven and transfer to a wire rack to cool for 1 hour. Decorate the exposed portion of the fruit with the rose petals. When the galette is at room temperature, slice and serve, ideally to be eaten out of hand at a picnic with a glass of rosé.

Store leftover galette, well wrapped in plastic wrap or under a pie dome, at room temperature for up to 2 days.

APRICOT PREP

Using a paring knife, hold an apricot in one hand and cut along the pit, starting at the stem end and moving to the bottom. Repeat the same cut ¼ inch from the first one. Press the paring knife into the slice, encouraging it to pop out. Continue until you're left with the pit, and transfer the slices to a mixing bowl. Repeat with the remaining apricots.

Northern Michigan is the cherry capital of the world, harvesting tens of thousands of tons each year. Down in the southeast corner of the state, we get the bright red fresh cherries for just two to three weeks in July. At the tail end of the season, our customers are devastated but the staff quietly rejoices when the cherry-pitting work days are over.

We do these tiny stone fruits justice with this Old Fashioned–inspired number: tart, bright red cherries are stirred, not shaken, with a big ol' splash of bourbon and a sprinkling of orange zest and turbinado sugar.

Prepping cherries is a pain and a half, but the paper clip method, while tedious, has never steered us wrong. If you're up for it, grab a pal you haven't seen in a spell and two bowls—one for the pits and one for the flesh. ♥

SOUR CHERRY BOURBON PIE

Makes one 9-inch pie

FILLING

2½ pounds sour cherries, stemmed and pitted (8 cups)

¼ cup bourbon of choice

½ teaspoon almond extract

¼ teaspoon packed grated orange zest

¾ cup turbinado sugar

¼ cup tapioca starch

¼ teaspoon kosher salt

1 disc All-Butter Pie Dough (page 25), rolled out and fitted into a 9-inch pie pan but uncrimped and refrigerated

6 lattice strips made from All-Butter Pie Dough (page 25), placed on a parchment-lined baking sheet and refrigerated

2 tablespoons cream cheese, at room temperature

2 tablespoons (¼ stick) unsalted butter, cubed and chilled

1 egg, beaten

1 tablespoon Sugar-Sugar (see page 12)

Make the filling: Place the cherries in a large mixing bowl and toss with the bourbon, almond extract, and orange zest. In a small bowl, combine the turbinado sugar with the tapioca starch and salt. Pour over the cherries and toss with your hands until evenly distributed.

Remove the unbaked crust and lattice strips from the refrigerator. Using a small offset spatula or the back of a spoon, evenly spread the cream cheese on the bottom of the pie shell. Layer the cherries on top of the cream cheese, being careful not to mound them in the center. Dot the filling with the butter cubes.

The lattice process is illustrated on page 53. Here is a brief description if you need a refresher. Place one strip of lattice across the center of the pie. Take another strip and lay it on top, perpendicular to the first one, creating a cross. Lay the next two strips on either side of the first strip you laid down, so they are parallel to both each other and the original strip. Next, working with the original strip, fold back both ends toward the center. Place the last two lattice strips down on either side of the second (perpendicular) strip. It should look like a woven lattice.

Tear the ends of the lattice pieces so they are flush with the perimeter of the tin. Roll the edge of the crust in, sealing the lattice. Crimp, using the technique described on page 49, being careful to push the crimps down and into the pie, as opposed to keeping them too loose on the edge. Put the assembled pie in the freezer for a 15-minute rest.

Preheat your oven to 450°F. Line a baking sheet with parchment paper.

Remove the pie from the freezer, place on the parchment-lined baking sheet, and brush the lattice and crimped edge with the beaten egg. Sprinkle the pie evenly with the Sugar-Sugar. Transfer the baking sheet with the pie on it to the oven and bake for 15 to 20 minutes, or until the crust is evenly golden brown. Turn the temperature down to 350°F and continue to bake for 1 to 1½ hours, until the pie juices are bubbling in the center.

Remove the baking sheet from the oven and transfer the pie to a wire rack to cool for 4 to 6 hours. When the pie is at room temperature, slice into 6 to 8 pieces and serve.

Store leftover pie, well wrapped in plastic wrap or under a pie dome, at room temperature for up to 2 days.

PITTING LIKE A PRO

The paperclip method for pitting cherries has never steered us wrong: Take a clean, silver paperclip (avoid ones with a plastic coating) and bend the inner hook all the way back so you have one long paperclip. Use whichever end you prefer and insert it into the cherry, grabbing onto the pit. Pull the paperclip out and voila! Now just a billion more to go. . .

When a farmer asks if you'd like to experiment with edible flower petals, you say yes! There's nothing quite like a culinary challenge to renew the creative spirit. Gwen, a friend and co-owner of Coriander Kitchen and Farm in Detroit, presented us with her treasure trove of calendula, marigolds, and bachelor buttons one summer. We first added them to salads before ordering them regularly to appear in numerous elements of our bright, tangy, and whimsical blueberry-rhubarb pie. ♥

BLUE-BARB BLOSSOM PIE

Makes one 9-inch pie

BLOSSOM CRUMBLE

¾ cup rolled oats

¾ cup all-purpose flour

⅓ cup packed light brown sugar

¼ teaspoon ground cinnamon

¼ teaspoon kosher salt

½ cup (1 stick) unsalted butter, straight from the fridge

FILLING

¾ cup granulated sugar

2 packed tablespoons mixed fresh edible flower petals (such as calendula, marigold, and bachelor button)

⅛ teaspoon ground allspice

⅛ teaspoon ground ginger

¼ teaspoon kosher salt

⅓ cup tapioca starch

1 pound blueberries, rinsed and picked over (3 cups)

1½ pounds rhubarb, trimmed and sliced into ½-inch pieces (4½ cups)

1 tablespoon freshly squeezed orange juice

Make the crumble: In a mixing bowl, combine the oats, flour, brown sugar, cinnamon, and salt and stir to mix well. Place the butter in the bowl and coat on all sides with the flour mixture. Take a bench scraper and cut the butter into ½-inch cubes directly into the flour mixture in the bowl. Work to break up the cubes with your hands until they are lightly coated with the flour mixture. Continue to use the bench scraper to cut the cubes into smaller pieces—the idea is that you are cutting each cube in half.

Switch to a pastry blender, and begin to cut in the butter with one hand while turning the bowl with the other. It's important not to aim for the same spot at the bottom of the bowl with each movement, but to actually slice through butter every time. You'll need to clean out the pastry blender every few turns of the bowl. Once most of the butter is incorporated, use your fingers to fully break down the butter until it is no longer visible. Be careful not to overwork the mixture at this point. The crumble may be completed up to 2 days ahead and stored in the fridge.

When you're ready to assemble and bake the pie, preheat your oven to 350°F. Line a baking sheet with parchment paper.

Make the filling: Place the sugar and flower petals in a food processor or spice grinder and pulse until the petals have broken down. Transfer to a large mixing bowl and combine with the allspice, ginger, salt, and tapioca starch. Add the blueberries, rhubarb, and orange juice and toss together with your hands or a spoon until thoroughly incorporated.

CONTINUED

2 tablespoons cream cheese, at room temperature

One 9-inch crust made with All-Butter Pie Dough (page 25), blind baked and cooled (page 50)

1 large egg, beaten

¼ cup mixed fresh edible flower petals (such as calendula, marigold, bachelor buttons)

Using a small offset spatula, evenly spread the cream cheese on the bottom of the pie shell. Brush the crimped edge with the beaten egg. Layer the blueberry-rhubarb filling on top of the cream cheese, being careful not to mound it in the center. Carefully cover the fruit with the crumble topping, leaving a small hole in the center of the pie, to serve both as a steam vent for the fruit as it cooks and as an indicator of when the pie is done. If the hole closes up during baking, insert a knife to bust it back open. Place the assembled pie on the parchment-lined baking sheet.

Transfer the baking sheet with the pie on it to the oven and bake for 70 to 90 minutes, until the pie juices begin to bubble in the center and the crumble topping is uniformly a deep golden color.

Remove the baking sheet from the oven and transfer the pie to a wire rack to cool for 4 to 6 hours. Decorate the baked pie with the flower petals or a few whole blossoms. When the pie is at room temperature, slice it into 6 to 8 pieces and serve.

Store leftover pie, well wrapped in plastic wrap or under a pie dome, at room temperature for up to 2 days.

While strawberries and balsamic vinegar have become a classic pairing, it's blueberries, plums, and balsamic that make us sing. The vinegar helps break down the fruit into a caramel-like, jammy filling with a syrupy-sweet texture. Use Balsamic Vinegar of Modena with an IGP designation for this pie—it can withstand heat and cooking for long periods of time. ♥

BLUEBERRY PLUM BALSAMIC PIE

Makes one 9-inch pie

FILLING

¼ cup turbinado sugar

¼ cup packed light brown sugar

2 teaspoons balsamic vinegar

⅛ teaspoon freshly ground black pepper

¼ teaspoon kosher salt

1¼ pounds blueberries, rinsed and picked over (4 cups)

1¾ pounds Stanley, Santa Rosa, or Early Golden plums, pluots, or a mixture, sliced (4 cups)

¼ cup tapioca starch

1 disc All-Butter Pie Dough (page 25), rolled out and fitted into a 9-inch pie pan but uncrimped and refrigerated

6 lattice strips made with All-Butter Pie Dough (page 25), placed on a parchment-lined baking sheet and refrigerated

2 tablespoons cream cheese, at room temperature

2 tablespoons (¼ stick) unsalted butter, cubed and chilled

1 large egg, beaten

1 tablespoon Sugar-Sugar (see page 12)

Make the filling: In a large bowl, combine the turbinado sugar, light brown sugar, balsamic vinegar, black pepper, and salt. Whisk until the mixture forms a wet paste, then add the blueberries, plums, and tapioca starch. Toss with your hands until thoroughly mixed.

Remove the unbaked crust and lattice strips from the refrigerator. Using a small offset spatula, evenly spread the cream cheese on the bottom of the pie shell. Layer the blueberry-plum mixture on top of the cream cheese, being careful not to mound it in the center. Dot the filling with the butter cubes.

The lattice process is illustrated on page 53. Here is a brief description if you need a refresher. Place one strip of lattice across the center of the pie. Take another strip and lay it on top, perpendicular to the first one, creating a cross. Lay the next two strips on either side of the first strip you laid down, so they are parallel to both each other and the original strip. Next, working with the original strip, fold back both ends toward the center, and then place the last two lattice strips down on either side of the second (perpendicular) strip. It should look like a woven lattice.

Tear the ends of lattice pieces so they are flush with the perimeter of the tin. Roll the edge of the crust in, sealing the lattice. Crimp as described on page 49, being careful to push the crimps down and into the pie, as opposed to keeping them too loose on the edge. Put the assembled pie in the freezer for a 15-minute rest.

Preheat your oven to 450°F. Line a baking sheet with parchment paper.

Remove the pie from the freezer, place on the parchment-lined baking sheet, and brush the lattice and crimped edge with the beaten egg. Sprinkle the pie evenly with the Sugar-Sugar.

CONTINUED

Transfer the baking sheet with the pie on it to the oven and bake for 15 to 20 minutes, until the crust is evenly golden brown. Lower the temperature to 350°F and continue to bake for 1 to 1½ hours, or until the pie juices are bubbling in the center.

Remove the baking sheet from the oven and transfer the pie to a wire rack to cool for 4 to 6 hours. When the pie is at room temperature, slice it into 6 to 8 pieces and serve.

Store leftover pie, well wrapped in plastic wrap or under a pie dome, at room temperature for up to 2 days.

All good pie bakers need a biscuit-topped pie in their repertoire. This one combines juicy, skin-on peaches with plenty of zingy fresh ginger and a warm cornmeal drop biscuit topping, all layered into a blind-baked all-butter crust. It's where shortcake meets pie and is surprisingly easy to pull together. You could skip the bottom crust altogether and it would still be a fantastic summer treat. ♥

GINGER PEACH BISCUIT PIE

Makes one 9-inch pie

FILLING

2 pounds ripe peaches, sliced (6 cups)

1 tablespoon packed freshly grated ginger

1 tablespoon freshly squeezed lemon juice

¼ cup tapioca starch

¼ cup granulated sugar

⅓ cup packed light brown sugar

¼ teaspoon kosher salt

BISCUIT TOPPING

1½ cups all-purpose flour

¾ cup fine yellow cornmeal

⅓ cup packed light brown sugar

1½ teaspoons baking powder

¼ teaspoon kosher salt

½ cup plus 2 tablespoons (1¼ sticks) unsalted butter, cubed and chilled

1 cup buttermilk, cold

2 tablespoons cream cheese, at room temperature

Make the filling: Place the peaches in a large mixing bowl and combine with the grated ginger and lemon juice. In a small bowl, combine the tapioca starch, granulated and brown sugars, and salt. Pour over the peaches and toss with your hands to distribute evenly.

Preheat your oven to 350°F. Line a baking sheet with parchment paper.

Make the biscuit topping: In a large bowl, combine the flour, cornmeal, brown sugar, baking powder, and salt and stir to mix well. Place the butter in the bowl and coat on all sides with the flour mixture. Take the bench scraper and cut the butter into ½-inch cubes directly into the flour mixture in the bowl. Work to break up the cubes with your hands until they are lightly coated with the flour mixture. Continue to use the bench scraper to cut the cubes into smaller pieces.

Switch to a pastry blender and use a rocking motion to cut in the butter with one hand while turning the bowl with the other. It's important not to aim for the same spot at the bottom of the bowl with each movement, but to actually slice through butter every time. Continue to blend and turn until most of the butter is incorporated but you still have quite a few larger chunks, as you would when making pie dough (page 25), but stopping before you get to the pea and Parmesan stage.

CONTINUED

One 9-inch crust made with All-Butter Pie Dough (page 25), extra blind baked and cooled (page 50)

1 large egg, beaten

Pour in the buttermilk and use a large silicone spatula to incorporate it into the flour-butter mixture, stopping when you don't see visible pools of liquid anymore. Switch to your hands, and scoop as many of the ingredients up as you can from the side of the bowl farthest from you, then press them down firmly onto the rest of the ingredients. Turn the bowl and repeat, scooping and turning until the dough comes completely together and no dry spots remain.

Using a small offset spatula, evenly spread the cream cheese on the bottom of the pie shell. Brush the crimped edge with the beaten egg. Layer the peach mixture on top of the cream cheese layer, being careful not to create a mound in the center. Carefully cover the fruit with the biscuit topping, leaving a small hole in the center of the pie to serve both as a steam vent for the fruit as it cooks and as an indicator of when the pie is done. Place the assembled pie on the parchment-lined baking sheet.

Transfer the baking sheet with the pie on it to the oven and bake for 30 minutes, then reduce the oven temperature to 325°F and continue to bake for 1 hour, or until the pie juices are beginning to bubble in the center and the biscuit topping is uniformly golden in color.

Remove the baking sheet from the oven and transfer the pie to a wire rack to cool for 4 to 6 hours. When the pie is at room temperature, slice it into 6 to 8 pieces and serve.

Store leftover pie, well wrapped in plastic wrap or under a pie dome, at room temperature for up to 2 days.

PEACH PREP

Using a paring knife, hold a peach in one hand and cut along the pit, starting at the stem end and moving to the bottom. Repeat that same cut ½ inch from the first one. Press the paring knife into the slice, encouraging it to pop out. Continue until you're left with the pit, and transfer the slices to a mixing bowl. Repeat with the remaining peaches.

Michigan's summer harvest is at its peak when the sweet corn and nectarines come to town. This pie is extra corny, with milky fresh kernels in the filling and prominent stone-ground cornmeal in the streusel to accompany the tart, sweet bites of nectarine. ♥

SWEET CORN NECTARINE STREUSEL PIE

Makes one 9-inch pie

STREUSEL

1 cup fine yellow cornmeal

½ cup all-purpose flour

⅓ cup packed light brown sugar

½ teaspoon kosher salt

7 tablespoons unsalted butter, straight from the fridge

FILLING

2 cups corn plus juices, fresh off the cob and coarsely chopped

⅓ cup granulated sugar

2½ pounds nectarines, cut into ½-inch chunks (4 cups)

1 tablespoon freshly squeezed lime juice

¼ cup tapioca starch

¼ teaspoon kosher salt

2 tablespoons cream cheese, at room temperature

One 9-inch crust made with All-Butter Pie Dough (page 25), blind baked and cooled (page 50)

1 large egg, beaten

Make the streusel: Combine the cornmeal, flour, brown sugar, and salt in a large bowl and stir to mix well. Place the butter in the bowl and coat on all sides with the flour mixture. Take a bench scraper and cut the butter into ½-inch cubes directly into the flour mixture in the bowl. Work to break up the cubes with your hands until they are lightly coated with the flour mixture. Continue to use the bench scraper to cut the cubes into smaller pieces.

Switch to a pastry blender and use a rocking motion to cut in the butter with one hand while turning the bowl with the other. It's important not to aim for the same spot at the bottom of the bowl with each movement, but to actually slice through butter every time. Once most of the butter is incorporated, use your fingers to fully break down the butter until the streusel resembles wet sand. Be careful not to overwork the mixture. The streusel can be made up to 2 days in advance and stored in the refrigerator.

When you're ready to assemble and bake the pie, preheat your oven to 350°F. Line a baking sheet with parchment paper.

Make the filling: In a food processor or blender, combine half of the corn kernels with the sugar and blend until it looks like creamed corn went one step too far, or until most of the corn is broken down. In a large bowl, gently combine the blended corn with the remaining corn, the nectarines, and the lime juice. In a small bowl, mix together the tapioca starch and salt. Pour over the corn and nectarines and toss with your hands until evenly distributed.

Using a small offset spatula, evenly spread the cream cheese on the bottom of the pie shell. Brush the crimped edge with the beaten egg. Layer the corn-nectarine mixture on top of the cream cheese, being careful not to mound it in the center. Carefully cover

CONTINUED

the fruit with the streusel topping, leaving a small hole in the center of the pie to serve both as a steam vent for the fruit as it cooks and as an indicator of when the pie is done. If the hole closes up during baking, insert a knife to bust it back open. Place the assembled pie on the parchment-lined baking sheet.

Transfer the baking sheet with the pie on it to the oven and bake for 1½ to 2 hours, until the pie juices are beginning to bubble in the center and the streusel topping is uniformly a deep golden color.

Remove the baking sheet from the oven, transfer the pie to a wire rack, and allow to cool for 4 to 6 hours. When the pie is at room temperature, slice it into 6 to 8 pieces and serve.

Store leftover pie, well wrapped in plastic wrap or under a pie dome, at room temperature for up to 2 days.

CORN PREP

Stand an ear of corn up in a large bowl with the skinnier end up. Use a very sharp knife to slice down right along the cob, removing the corn as you go. Once the corn has been released into the bowl, run your knife upward in the opposite direction to release the milky residue, and place that back in the bowl with the corn. Repeat until all of the corn kernels are removed. This should yield between ¾ and 1 cups corn.

NECTARINE PREP

With a chef's knife, slice each nectarine along the pit into four pieces. Set the pieces face down on a cutting board and cut each into ½-inch chunks.

The cooler months lead to frigid weather in Detroit, and there's pie every skip of the way. We enjoy the harvest bounty with plums, then move on to grapes, apples, squash, and cranberries before eventually settling in a no-fresh-fruit zone. Our seasonal traditions at the shop are just as significant as the pie. In the fall, we close our doors to take the staff on an apple-picking day, complete with bumpy tractor ride, cider slushies, warm cinnamon doughnuts, and big bags filled with our Northern Spy haul. We decorate with autumnal gourd gusto and get heavy into Thanksgiving-prep mode, making extra pie dough during every shift and marking off each round on the running tally. December turns us into cookie-baking wizards for one big final push before the new year. Then the slowness of winter settles in, and we're content to hang near the ovens all the livelong day.

You can find Concord grape vines all over Brooklyn, and every time I passed one while I was living there, I'd think about the potential for pie. I was filming an episode a week for my cooking show when I first made this pie, embracing every chance to try something new. At first, I added the goat cheese to the crust, but I have subsequently learned that it's much more powerful laid underneath the filling. It's like an all-inclusive wine and cheese party. ♥

CONCORD GRAPE AND GOAT CHEESE PIE

Makes one 9-inch pie

FILLING

2 pounds Concord grapes, stemmed (approximately 7½ cups)

1 teaspoon freshly squeezed lemon juice

⅔ cup granulated sugar

¼ cup tapioca starch

¼ teaspoon kosher salt

1 disc All-Butter Pie Dough (page 25), rolled out into a 10-inch round and laid flat on a parchment-lined baking sheet and refrigerated

1 disc All-Butter Pie Dough (page 25), rolled out and fitted into a 9-inch pie pan but uncrimped and refrigerated

2 ounces goat cheese, at room temperature

2 tablespoons (¼ stick) unsalted butter, cubed and chilled

1 large egg, beaten

Make the filling: Gently squeeze the pulp from each grape, and set the skins aside. Place all of the pulp in a heavy-bottomed saucepan over medium heat, and cook for 5 to 6 minutes, just until the seeds start to separate from the pulp. Set a fine-mesh strainer over a mixing bowl. Transfer the cooked grapes to the strainer and press the mixture through the strainer as completely as possible. Carefully remove the seeds from the pulp with a spoon so that you can still use the pulp that will not fit through the strainer. Combine the pulp and skins in a large bowl. Add the lemon juice, sugar, tapioca starch, and salt. Mix it up!

When you're ready to assemble the pie, remove the unbaked crusts from the refrigerator. Crumble the goat cheese evenly all over the bottom of the pie shell. Flatten with the back of a spoon, and layer the grape mixture on top. Dot the grapes with the butter cubes. Place the second crust on top.

The crimping process is shown on page 48. Here is a brief description if you need a refresher: Roll the dough overhang of the bottom crust toward the center of the pie, creating a ring of dough, as though you were rolling a poster tightly. Roll the dough with one thumb while the other thumb presses the dough down into the tin's edge to seal. Then form a "C" with the thumb and index finger of one hand and use those fingers to pinch and lift the rim of the dough up and away from the pan, simultaneously pressing the thumb of your other hand into the "C" to make a crimp. Continue until the entire ring of dough is crimped. Put the assembled pie in the freezer for a 15-minute rest.

CONTINUED

Preheat your oven to 450°F. Line a baking sheet with parchment paper.

Remove the pie from the freezer, place on the parchment-lined baking sheet, and brush the top and crimped edge with the beaten egg. Use a paring knife to cut steam vents in whatever design you like (see page 102). Transfer the baking sheet with the pie on it to the oven and bake for 15 to 20 minutes, until the crust is evenly golden brown. Lower the temperature to 325°F and continue to bake for 50 to 70 minutes, until the pie juices are bubbling in the center.

Remove the baking sheet from the oven and transfer the pie to a wire rack to cool for 4 to 6 hours. When the pie is at room temperature, slice it into 6 to 8 pieces and serve.

Store leftover pie, well wrapped in plastic wrap or under a pie dome, at room temperature for up to 2 days.

Plum pie is traditionally considered a winter holiday treat, but our plum farmer brings us these tart, jammy stone fruits in August and September, so we embrace that ritual and celebrate a harvest holiday instead. The brown butter, oats, and spices create a pie that is comforting and warm in flavor, making for an easier transition from the summer sun to the autumn breeze. Stanley plums are those recognizable, classic purple plums and they're great for this pie. However, an assortment of plums makes for a gorgeous filling and complex fruit flavor. If you come across Santa Rosas, Early Goldens, or even pluots (a plum-apricot hybrid) at the market, throw them into the mix! Serve this pie with thick, plain yogurt if you know what's good for you. ♥

BROWN BUTTER PLUM CRUMBLE PIE

Makes one 9-inch pie

CRUMBLE

12 tablespoons (1½ sticks) unsalted butter, straight from the fridge

1 cup rolled oats

½ cup packed light brown sugar

1 cup all-purpose flour

⅛ teaspoon freshly ground black pepper

½ teaspoon ground cinnamon

½ teaspoon kosher salt

FILLING

3 pounds Stanley, Santa Rosa, or Early Golden plums, pluots, or a mixture, sliced (7 cups)

Juice of ½ lemon

¼ cup turbinado sugar

¼ cup granulated sugar

¼ teaspoon kosher salt

¼ cup tapioca starch

2 tablespoons cream cheese, at room temperature

One 9-inch crust made with All-Butter Pie Dough (page 25), blind baked and cooled (page 50)

1 large egg, beaten

Make the crumble: Place the butter in a heavy-bottomed saucepan over medium heat, and use a silicone spatula to stir it gently occasionally. Swirl the pan every once in a while to distribute the heat evenly. You'll see the butter fully melt and separate, then start to boil. It will typically go through two phases of boiling: first a clear, almost fluorescent, foam will form, followed by a soapy, white foam. Tiny brown specks will then appear, marking the first signs of browning. Keep stirring, and do not leave unattended. The color will change from yellow to golden to a deep, toasted brown (similar to the color of beef stock or cola). If you're having trouble seeing the color beneath the foam, spoon a little into a clear glass and check. Set aside to cool slightly.

Carefully pour the brown butter into a liquid measuring cup or small tin and transfer to the fridge to fully return to its original temperature and solid form, about 2 hours. This step may be completed up to 4 days ahead; keep the brown butter stored in the fridge. When ready to use, loosen the butter by cutting around the edge with a paring knife, then invert the container and the butter should easily pop out. Cut the browned butter into ½-inch cubes.

In a mixing bowl, combine the oats, brown sugar, flour, pepper, cinnamon, and salt. Add the cold brown butter cubes and use a bench scraper to incorporate them into the dry mixture. Switch to a pastry blender and work the mixture to break down the butter into smaller pieces. Once most of the butter is incorporated, use your hands to fully incorporate the butter by gathering clumps in your fingertips and using a quick smearing motion to combine. When the crumble is done, you will not see any visible butter

BROWN BUTTER BEST PRACTICES

You'll want a game plan for this recipe, since it requires one extra step: browning the butter until your kitchen is filled with the most intoxicating aroma and then chilling the butter until it reverts to its solid form. I suggest you brown the butter when you make the pie dough, which also requires a rest in the fridge. However, I wouldn't recommend doing these steps simultaneously. Just ask anyone who works at Sister Pie: every time I've tried to multitask and make brown butter while doing something else, I've ended up with burnt butter.

chunks. The crumble may be completed up to 2 days ahead and stored in the fridge.

When you are ready to bake the pie, preheat the oven to 350°F. Line a baking sheet with parchment paper.

Make the filling: In a large mixing bowl, toss the plums and lemon juice together with your hands. In another bowl, mix the turbinado and granulated sugars, salt, and tapioca starch. Add to the plums and toss with your hands until evenly distributed.

Using a small offset spatula, evenly spread the cream cheese on the bottom of the pie shell. Brush the crimped edge with the beaten egg. Layer the plums on top of the cream cheese, being careful not to mound them in the center. Carefully cover the fruit with the crumble topping, leaving a small hole in the center of the pie to serve both as a steam vent for the fruit as it cooks and as an indicator of when the pie is done. If the hole closes up during baking, insert a knife to bust it back open. Place the assembled pie on the parchment-lined baking sheet.

Transfer the baking sheet with the pie on it to the oven and bake the pie for 70 to 90 minutes, until the pie juices are beginning to bubble in the center and the crumble topping is a uniformly deep golden color.

Remove the baking sheet from the oven and transfer the pie to a wire rack to cool for 4 to 6 hours. When the pie is at room temperature, slice it into 6 to 8 pieces and serve.

Store leftover pie, well wrapped in plastic wrap or under a pie dome, at room temperature for up to 2 days.

The combination of fruit and cheese dates back to ancient times, and we're keeping the tradition alive with our slightly savory apple pies. You can find a recipe for Apple Cheddar Rye Hand Pies on page 139, or try your hand at this one.

Every apple wants to be a baking apple, and the number of choices is downright overwhelming. What you want is an apple that won't shrink too much, maintains a firm texture, and is not too syrupy-sweet in flavor. We've had good luck with Golden Delicious, Jonagold, Granny Smith, and Idared. You can mix them, but we've had the best results when we stick with one type to achieve a consistent, even texture throughout the pie. ♥

APPLE SAGE GOUDA PIE

Makes one 9-inch pie

FILLING

2 pounds Northern Spy, Idared, or Golden Delicious apples, peeled and sliced

1 teaspoon freshly squeezed lemon juice

¾ cup granulated sugar

2 tablespoons minced fresh sage

¼ cup packed light brown sugar

¼ cup tapioca starch

¼ teaspoon ground cinnamon

½ teaspoon ground nutmeg

¼ teaspoon kosher salt

1 disc Aged Gouda Pie Dough (page 32), rolled out and fitted into a 9-inch pie pan but uncrimped, and refrigerated

6 lattice strips (page 52) made with Aged Gouda Pie Dough, placed on a parchment-lined baking sheet and refrigerated

1 teaspoon turbinado sugar mixed with 1 teaspoon all-purpose flour

Make the filling: Transfer the apples to a large mixing bowl and toss with the lemon juice.

In a medium bowl, combine the granulated sugar and sage, massaging together with your fingertips. Add the brown sugar, tapioca starch, cinnamon, nutmeg, and salt. Add to the apples and toss with your hands until evenly distributed.

When you're ready to assemble the pie, remove the unbaked crust and lattice strips from the refrigerator. Sprinkle the sugar-flour mixture all over the bottom of the crust. Layer the apples on top, being careful not to mound them in the center. Dot the apples with butter cubes.

The lattice process is illustrated on page 53. Here is a brief description if you need a refresher. Place one strip of lattice across the center of the pie. Take another strip and lay it on top, perpendicular to the first one, creating a cross. Lay the next two strips on either side of the first strip you laid down, so they are parallel to both each other and the original strip. Next, working with the original strip, fold back both ends toward the center, and then place the last two lattice strips down on either side of the second (perpendicular) strip. Fold the original strip back down, so that it lies across and on top of the newly placed strips. It should look like a woven lattice.

CONTINUED

2 tablespoons (¼ stick) unsalted butter, cubed and chilled

1 large egg, beaten

Tear off the ends of the lattice pieces so they are flush with the perimeter of the tin. Roll the edge of the crust in, sealing the lattice. Crimp, using the technique described on page 49, being careful to push the crimps down and into the pie, as opposed to keeping them too loose on the edge. Put the assembled pie in the freezer for a 15-minute rest.

Preheat your oven to 450°F. Line a baking sheet with parchment paper.

Remove the pie from the freezer, place on the baking sheet, and brush the lattice and crimped edge with the beaten egg. Transfer the baking sheet with the pie on it to the oven and bake for 15 to 20 minutes, or until the crust is evenly golden brown. Turn the temperature down to 325°F and continue to bake for 50 to 70 minutes, until the pie juices are bubbling in the center.

Remove the baking sheet from the oven and transfer the pie to a wire rack to cool for 4 to 6 hours. When the pie is at room temperature, slice it into 6 to 8 pieces and serve.

Store leftover pie, well wrapped in plastic wrap or under a pie dome, at room temperature for up to 2 days.

APPLE PREP

Use a peeler to remove the skin from the apples. With a chef's knife, slice each apple along the core into four pieces. Set the pieces face down on a cutting board and cut each into ¼-inch slices.

Asking me which pie is my favorite is like asking me if I'd rather dance to New Order or Mariah Carey—it's impossible to choose. But if I had to pick just one pie, it'd be this Sister Pie classic, because it lives up to my formula of what creates the ultimate pie experience: flaky, all-butter crust meets the tartest fruit in season plus a buttery, brown sugar crumble topping. It features tart Michigan cranberries in two ways: first we cook them down into a compote and then we mix in more cranberries, sugar, and spice. The whole darn thing is topped with the aforementioned crumble, and we're in (best pie) business.

We use cranberries from Cheboygan, Michigan. They're sold in 12-ounce bags at most supermarkets during the fall and winter season. It also may be possible to find unbagged cranberries at your local farmers' market or grocery store. While rinsing, be sure to sort the cranberries as well and remove any that appear mushy or dark.

The first two components of this recipe—the compote and the crumble—can be made up to 4 days in advance and stored in the refrigerator until you're ready to make the pie. ♥

CRANBERRY CRUMBLE PIE

Makes one 9-inch pie

COMPOTE

12 ounces cranberries, rinsed and sorted

¼ cup plus 2 tablespoons packed light brown sugar

¾ teaspoon grated orange zest

1 tablespoon freshly squeezed orange juice

CRUMBLE

1 cup rolled oats

½ cup packed light brown sugar

1 cup all-purpose flour

½ teaspoon ground cinnamon

½ teaspoon kosher salt

½ cup plus 2 tablespoons (1¼ sticks) unsalted butter, straight from the fridge

First, make the compote: Combine the cranberries, brown sugar, and orange zest and juice in a heavy-bottomed saucepan. Cook over low to medium heat until the cranberries begin to burst. Remove from the heat and set aside to cool completely (or set in the freezer for a quick chill) while you continue to work. This compote can be made up to 4 days in advance and stored in the fridge until you're ready to use it.

Next, make the crumble: In a mixing bowl, combine the oats, brown sugar, flour, cinnamon, and salt. Place the butter in the bowl and coat on all sides with the flour mixture. Take a bench scraper and cut the butter into ½-inch cubes directly into the flour mixture in the bowl. Work to break up the cubes with your hands until they are lightly coated with the flour mixture. Continue to use the bench scraper to cut the cubes into smaller pieces—the idea is that you are cutting each cube in half.

Switch to a pastry blender and begin to cut in the butter with one hand while turning the bowl with the other. It's important not to aim for the same spot at the bottom of the bowl with each movement, but to actually slice through butter every time. You'll

CONTINUED

FILLING

¾ cup granulated sugar

¾ teaspoon ground cinnamon

1 teaspoon ground nutmeg

½ teaspoon ground allspice

¼ cup tapioca starch

1½ teaspoons kosher salt

8 ounces cranberries, rinsed and sorted

½ Bosc or D'Anjou pear, peeled and grated

2 tablespoons cream cheese, at room temperature

One 9-inch crust made with All-Butter Pie Dough (page 25), blind baked and cooled (page 50)

1 large egg, beaten

Vanilla ice cream, for serving (optional)

need to clean out the pastry blender every few turns of the bowl. Once most of the butter is incorporated, use your fingers to fully break down the butter until it is no longer visible. Be careful not to overwork the mixture at this point. The crumble can be completed up to 4 days ahead and stored in the fridge.

When you're ready to bake the pie, preheat your oven to 350°F. Line a baking sheet with parchment paper.

Make the filling: In a mixing bowl, combine the sugar, cinnamon, nutmeg, allspice, tapioca starch, and salt. Add the cranberries, pear, and cooled compote and use your hands or a wooden spoon to mix completely.

Using a small offset spatula, evenly spread the cream cheese on the bottom of the pie shell. Brush the crimped edge with the beaten egg. Layer the cranberry mixture on top of cream cheese—it should be evenly spread up to the bottom of the crimps. Carefully cover the fruit with the crumble topping, leaving a small hole in the center of the pie to serve both as a steam vent for the fruit as it cooks and as an indicator of when the pie is done. (In the photograph on the opposite page, the pie is not yet fully topped with the crumble.) Place the assembled pie on the parchment-lined baking sheet.

Transfer the baking sheet with the pie on it to the oven and bake for 60 to 70 minutes, until the pie juices are beginning to bubble in the center and the crumble topping is a uniformly deep golden color.

Remove the baking sheet from the oven and transfer the pie to a wire rack to cool for 4 to 6 hours. When the pie is at room temperature, slice it into 6 to 8 pieces. Serve with a big scoop of classic vanilla ice cream (technically, it's not my favorite pie unless it's served this way).

Store leftover pie, well wrapped in plastic wrap or under a pie dome, at room temperature for up to 2 days.

When they see this pie on our menu, most people wonder whether it is sweet or savory. Once you take a bite, you'll quickly recognize that it's a dessert pie, as it manages to hit a variety of flavors without going overboard: tangy from the cream cheese, warm from the cardamom, nutty and rich from the tahini and walnuts, and sweet from the roasted winter squash puree. Achieving all that nuance and depth involves some steps. Try not to be intimidated! You can make the tahini-walnut paste, the cardamom cream, and the winter squash a few days in advance.

We include a bit of canned pumpkin in our squash mix for that irreplaceably smooth texture. You'll likely be left with a little bit extra of each, as cans of pumpkin contain more than the needed amount and your squash yield could vary slightly. What to do with the remainder? Place it in a tightly sealed plastic bag and freeze for future pie. ♥

CARDAMOM TAHINI SQUASH PIE

Makes one 9-inch pie

WINTER SQUASH PUREE FILLING

2 pounds butternut, Hubbard, Buttercup, or acorn squash, or a mixture

2 tablespoons (¼ stick) unsalted butter, melted

2 tablespoons packed light brown sugar

½ cup canned pumpkin

1 cup heavy cream

1 tablespoon whole cardamom pods

½ cup packed light brown sugar

½ teaspoon ground cinnamon

½ teaspoon ground cardamom

½ teaspoon ground ginger

½ teaspoon ground allspice

1 tablespoon fine yellow cornmeal

1 teaspoon kosher salt

3 large eggs, at room temperature

1 teaspoon pure vanilla extract

Make the filling: Preheat your oven to 400°F. Line a baking sheet with parchment paper. Using a very sharp knife, halve the squash and hollow out the seedy center with a spoon. Place the squash cut sides up on the baking sheet. Brush generously with the melted butter and sprinkle evenly with the brown sugar. Bake for 1 hour, until the flesh is soft and cooked through. Remove the baking sheet from the oven and set it on a wire rack to cool. Once the squash has cooled, peel away the skin and add the flesh to a food processor with the pumpkin puree (you could also use an immersion blender for this step). Blend until well incorporated. Measure out 1½ cups for the pie filling. Keep the rest for another use. This puree can be made up to 2 days in advance and stored in the fridge. Remove from the fridge and let come to room temperature before completing the filling.

In a small saucepan, bring the cream to a gentle simmer. Remove from the heat, add the cardamom pods, and cover tightly with plastic wrap or a lid. Steep for 20 minutes, then remove and discard the cardamom pods. Let the cream cool to room temperature before using.

In a mixing bowl, whisk the brown sugar, cinnamon, ground cardamom, ginger, allspice, cornmeal, and salt. In another bowl, combine the eggs with the cardamom cream, the 1½ cups reserved squash puree, and the vanilla and whisk until smooth. Slowly pour the egg mixture into the brown sugar mixture and whisk until combined.

TAHINI-WALNUT PASTE

5 tablespoons finely ground toasted walnuts (see page 000)

2½ tablespoons tahini

2½ tablespoons packed light brown sugar

2½ tablespoons cream cheese, at room temperature

¼ teaspoon kosher salt

One 9-inch crust made with All-Butter Pie Dough (page 25), extra blind baked and cooled (page 50)

1 large egg, beaten

1 teaspoon sesame seeds, toasted (see page 35)

Whipped cream (see page 55), for serving

Make the tahini-walnut paste: Clean the bowl of the food processor and then add the walnuts, tahini, brown sugar, cream cheese, and salt and blend until smooth. This mixture can be made up to 2 days in advance and stored in the fridge. Remove from the fridge and let come to room temperature before assembling the pie.

When you're ready to bake the pie, preheat your oven to 325°F. Line a baking sheet with parchment paper.

Spoon the tahini-walnut paste onto the bottom of the crust, and spread evenly; use your fingers or the bottom of a measuring cup to pat it down. Brush the crimped edge with the beaten egg. Pour the squash filling into the pie shell until it reaches the bottom of the crimps. Place the assembled pie on the parchment-lined baking sheet.

Transfer the baking sheet with the pie on it to the oven and bake for 40 to 50 minutes, until the edges are puffed and the center jiggles only slightly when shaken. Remove the baking sheet from the oven and transfer the pie to a wire rack to cool for 4 to 6 hours. When the pie is at room temperature, sprinkle the sesame seeds on top and slice it into 6 to 8 pieces. Serve with cold freshly whipped cream and a drizzle of tahini—even though I don't like the word "drizzle."

Store leftover pie, well wrapped in plastic wrap, in the refrigerator for up to 2 days.

It was an adjustment for my family when I started bringing pies to Thanksgiving dinner. My grandmother Mimi's pumpkin pies have been the mainstay at our holiday gathering since well before my time on this earth. Made with a can of evaporated milk and baked in scalloped metal pie tins with her name etched on the bottom of each one, they evoke tradition like no other food can. Throughout the years, my mom, Aunt Sue, and I have experimented with various stuffings, pumpkin fondues, and turkey-roasting styles. Heck, we even introduced cider-glazed brussels sprouts to the menu a few years back (it was a big deal). The crew seems generally excited for these menu updates, but one thing is crystal clear: the pumpkin pie must never change.

Here at Sister Pie, we've decided that our pumpkin pies should tread the line between traditional and nouveau. If you've chosen to join the line down the block at 6 AM on a cold November morning, you're doing it because you want an interesting, delicious, and, yes, crowd-pleasing pie. This Buttermilk Pumpkin Streusel Pie achieves just that. A slightly tangy, super-creamy pumpkin filling is baked in our all-butter pie shell and then topped with a nutty buckwheat streusel for a perfect butter crunch. The greatest part about the streusel topping? It covers any unsightly cracks that might occur while the pie bakes! ♥

BUTTERMILK PUMPKIN STREUSEL PIE

Makes one 9-inch pie

BUCKWHEAT PEPITA STREUSEL TOPPING

½ cup all-purpose flour

¼ cup buckwheat flour

¼ cup pepitas, toasted (see page 35)

1 teaspoon ground cinnamon

¼ cup packed light brown sugar

¼ teaspoon kosher salt

½ cup (1 stick) unsalted butter, straight from the fridge

Preheat your oven to 325°F. Line two baking sheets with parchment paper.

Make the streusel topping: In a mixing bowl, combine the all-purpose and buckwheat flours, pepitas, cinnamon, brown sugar, and salt. Place the butter in the bowl and coat on all sides with the flour mixture. Take a bench scraper and cut the butter into ½-inch cubes directly into the flour mixture in the bowl. Work to break up the cubes with your hands until they are lightly coated with the flour mixture. Continue to use the bench scraper to cut the cubes into smaller pieces—the idea is that you are cutting each cube in half.

Switch to a pastry blender and begin to cut in the butter with one hand while turning the bowl with the other. It's important not to aim for the same spot at the bottom of the bowl with each movement, but to actually slice through butter every time. You'll need to clean out the pastry blender every few turns of the bowl. Once most of the butter is incorporated, use your fingers to fully break down the butter until it is no longer visible. Be careful not to overwork the mixture at this point. Scatter the streusel over one of the parchment-lined baking sheets, distributing it evenly, and

FILLING

1 (15-ounce) can pumpkin puree

¾ cup buttermilk, at room temperature

3 large eggs, at room temperature

2 tablespoons Grade B maple syrup

2 tablespoons (¼ stick) unsalted butter, melted and cooled

2 tablespoons fine yellow cornmeal

¾ cup packed light brown sugar

½ teaspoon kosher salt

½ teaspoon ground cinnamon

½ teaspoon ground ginger

One 9-inch crust made with All-Butter Pie Dough (page 25), extra blind baked and cooled (page 50)

1 large egg, beaten

transfer the baking sheet to the oven. Bake for approximately 25 minutes, gently tossing the mixture with a spatula about halfway through. When the streusel is evenly browned and does not appear wet anymore, remove the baking sheet from the oven. Cool completely on a wire rack.

Make the filling: In a mixing bowl, combine the pumpkin, buttermilk, eggs, syrup, melted butter, cornmeal, brown sugar, salt, cinnamon, and ginger and whisk until well blended.

Place the blind-baked shell on the other parchment-lined baking sheet. Brush the crimped edge with the beaten egg. Pour the buttermilk-pumpkin filling into the pie shell until it reaches the bottom of the crimps. Transfer the baking sheet with the pie on it to the oven and bake for 50 to 60 minutes, until the edges are puffed and the center jiggles only slightly when shaken.

Remove the baking sheet from the oven and transfer the pie to a wire rack. Let cool for 15 minutes, then cover the pie with the streusel topping. Allow the pie to fully cool and set for another 4 to 6 hours. When the pie is at room temperature, slice it into 6 to 8 pieces and serve.

Store leftover pie, well wrapped in plastic wrap, in the refrigerator for up to 2 days.

Before I started making pie for a living, I don't remember trying pecan pie. I thought the corn syrupy sweetness would be a turnoff. How can you taste the flavor with all that sugar? There's a simple fix to that, and I'm certainly not the first to figure it out: add booze! We use 80 proof, 7½-year-old Laird's Apple Brandy with notes of cardamom, tobacco, and toffee. We replace the corn syrup altogether with Grade B maple syrup and a little honey. The pie is extra nutty thanks to a big pile of toasted whole pecans in the filling, plus we toast and grind pecans for an alternative crust. We keep coming back to it for a reason. ♥

BRANDY PECAN PIE

Makes one 9-inch pie

FILLING

⅔ cup turbinado sugar

¼ cup (½ stick) unsalted butter, cubed

½ cup Grade B maple syrup

¼ cup honey

2 tablespoons fine yellow cornmeal

3 large eggs, at room temperature

1 teaspoon pure vanilla extract

2 tablespoons apple brandy

½ teaspoon kosher salt

One 9-inch crust made with Toasted Pecan Pie Dough (page 25), extra blind baked and cooled (see page 50)

1 teaspoon turbinado sugar mixed with 1 teaspoon all-purpose flour

1½ cups whole pecans, toasted (see page 35)

1 large egg, beaten

Unsweetened whipped cream, for serving (optional)

Preheat your oven to 325°F.

Make the filling: Place the turbinado sugar and cubed butter in a small, heatproof bowl. Combine the maple syrup and honey in a small, heavy-bottomed saucepan and slowly bring to a boil. Continue boiling until the mixture reads 225°F on a candy thermometer. Pour the maple-honey mixture over the turbinado sugar and butter and stir until the butter has completely melted. Whisk in the cornmeal. Set aside to cool slightly.

In a separate bowl, whisk the eggs with the vanilla, brandy, and salt.

Slowly pour the cooled butter mixture into the egg mixture, whisking constantly.

Place the blind-baked pecan crust on a parchment-lined baking sheet. Sprinkle the bottom of the crust with the turbinado sugar–flour mixture, then spread the toasted pecans evenly on top. Brush the crimped edge with the beaten egg. Carefully pour in the filling until it reaches the bottom of the crimps. Use a knife or fork to poke down any pecans that aren't submerged in the filling.

Transfer the baking sheet with the pie on it to the oven and bake for 40 to 50 minutes, or until puffed around the edges and only slightly jiggly in the center when shaken.

Remove the baking sheet from the oven and transfer the pie to a wire rack to cool for 4 to 6 hours. When the pie is at room temperature, slice it into 6 to 8 pieces. Serve with whipped cream.

Store leftover pie, well wrapped in plastic wrap or under a pie dome, at room temperature for up to 2 days.

Pies with chocolate, candied ginger, and even candy canes (no joke) have all had their turn on the menu. Our Pfeffernusse Pie is inspired by a traditional German holiday cookie of the same name, which translates literally to "pepper nuts," although most recipes don't have nuts in them at all. Over the years, the cookie has evolved much like a story in a game of telephone. The version of pfeffernusse we love are deeply spiced molasses cookies, soft on the inside with a firm exterior. A dunk in powdered sugar after baking makes them look like little snowballs. One bite of the creamy, gingerbread-like filling and you're just gosh darn consumed with holiday cheer. ♥

PFEFFERNUSSE PIE

Makes one 9-inch pie

FILLING

½ cup (1 stick) unsalted butter, melted and cooled

¼ cup dark molasses

¾ cup packed light brown sugar

¼ cup fine yellow cornmeal

½ teaspoon kosher salt

3 large eggs, at room temperature

¾ cup heavy cream, at room temperature

1 teaspoon pure vanilla extract

⅛ teaspoon freshly ground black pepper

⅛ teaspoon ground cardamom

⅛ teaspoon ground ginger

⅛ teaspoon ground cinnamon

⅛ teaspoon ground cloves

⅛ teaspoon ground nutmeg

One 9-inch crust made with All-Butter Pie Dough (page 25), blind baked and cooled (page 50)

1 large egg, beaten

Powdered sugar, for dusting

Preheat your oven to 350°F. Line a baking sheet with parchment paper.

Make the filling: Combine the melted butter with the molasses in a mixing bowl. Whisk in the brown sugar, cornmeal, and salt.

Crack the eggs into a medium bowl. Add the cream, vanilla, pepper, cardamom, ginger, cinnamon, cloves, and nutmeg and whisk until combined. Slowly pour the egg mixture into the molasses mixture and whisk until combined.

Place the blind-baked crust on the parchment-lined baking sheet. Brush the crimped edge with the beaten egg. Carefully pour in the filling until it reaches the bottom of the crimps.

Transfer the baking sheet with the pie on it to the oven and bake for 40 to 50 minutes, or until puffed around the edges and only slightly jiggly in the center when shaken.

Remove the baking sheet from the oven and transfer the pie to a wire rack to cool for 4 to 6 hours. Once it is completely cool, use a sifter to dust a layer of powdered sugar on top of the pie. When the pie is at room temperature, slice it into 6 to 8 pieces and serve.

Store leftover pie, well wrapped in plastic wrap or under a pie dome, at room temperature for up to 2 days.

A mincemeat pie at Christmastime has been on the long list of customer requests since before we even opened the bakery doors. At its inception in Britain back in the seventeenth century, mincemeat pie was traditionally filled with minced meat, beef suet, dried fruit, and spices. Over time, the pie became sweeter, lost the meat, and kept the beef suet. Like fruitcake, mincemeat filling is aged to allow the flavors to blend and mellow. A quick three-day rest suits this pie well, but you're welcome to age it longer, depending on your appetite for risk!

We're a vegetarian bakery 99 percent of the time, so our take on mincemeat pie is certainly not traditional and features no beef suet. Instead, we combine chopped pears—we prefer Bosc or D'Anjou for baking—and nuts, with dried fruits, spices, booze, and maple to Sister Pie it up. ♥

MINCED PEAR PIE

Makes one 9-inch pie

FILLING

3 pears, peeled, cored, and diced into ½-inch chunks

¼ cup finely chopped dried apricots

½ cup golden raisins

½ cup roughly chopped toasted walnuts (see page 35)

½ cup roughly chopped toasted pistachios

¼ cup finely chopped candied ginger

Juice and grated zest of 2 lemons

½ teaspoon ground cardamom

½ teaspoon ground ginger

¼ teaspoon ground cloves

¼ teaspoon ground allspice

½ teaspoon kosher salt

½ cup apple brandy

½ cup Grade B maple syrup

¼ cup tapioca starch

Make the filling: Combine the pears, apricots, raisins, walnuts, pistachios, candied ginger, lemon juice and zest, cardamom, ground ginger, cloves, allspice, salt, and brandy in a large bowl. In a liquid measuring cup, whisk together the maple syrup and tapioca starch, then pour it over the pear mixture. Use your hands or a spoon to toss until thoroughly combined. Cover the mixture with plastic wrap, or transfer to an airtight container, and age the filling in the refrigerator for at least 3 days and up to a year.

When you're ready to assemble the pie, remove the unbaked crusts from the refrigerator. Sprinkle the bottom of the pie shell with the turbinado sugar–flour mixture and spread the aged pear mixture on top. Dot the mixture with the butter cubes. Place the second crust on top.

The crimping process is illustrated on page 53. Here is a brief description if you need a refresher. Roll the dough overhang of the bottom crust toward the center of the pie, creating a ring of dough, as though you were rolling a poster tightly. Roll the dough with one thumb while the other thumb presses the dough down into the tin's edge to seal. Then form a "C" with the thumb and index finger of one hand and use those fingers to pinch and lift the rim of the dough up and away from the pan, simultaneously pressing the thumb of your other hand into the "C" to make a crimp. Continue until the entire ring of dough is crimped. Put the assembled pie in the freezer for a 15-minute rest.

CONTINUED

1 disc All-Butter Pie Dough (page 25), rolled out into a 10-inch circle and laid flat on a parchment-lined baking sheet and refrigerated

1 disc All-Butter Pie Dough (page 25), rolled out and fitted into a 9-inch pie pan but uncrimped and refrigerated

1 teaspoon turbinado sugar mixed with 1 teaspoon all-purpose flour

2 tablespoons (¼ stick) unsalted butter, cubed and chilled

1 large egg, beaten

Preheat your oven to 450°F. Line a baking sheet with parchment paper.

Remove the pie from the freezer, place on the parchment-lined baking sheet, and brush the top and crimped edge with the beaten egg. Use a paring knife to cut steam vents in whatever design you like. Transfer the baking sheet with the pie on it to the oven and bake for 15 to 20 minutes, until the crust is evenly golden brown. Lower the temperature to 325°F and continue to bake for 50 to 70 minutes, until the pie juices are bubbling in the center.

Remove the baking sheet from the oven and transfer the pie to a wire rack to cool for 4 to 6 hours. When the pie is at room temperature, slice it into 6 to 8 pieces and serve.

Store leftover pie, well wrapped in plastic wrap or under a pie dome, at room temperature for up to 2 days.

GETTING FANCY WITH STEAM VENTS

Steam vents are decorations with a purpose—they dress-up your double-crust pie and let out the steam that juicy fruit pies create while baking, ensuring your top crust stays crisp all the way through. Make designs with a knife tip or cutter: Once you've placed the top crust on a pie and completed the crimping, take a sharp paring knife and insert the tip through the crust to make your design. Think about sewing stitches for inspiration. If you want to get fancier, use a small cutter to make punch-outs right after you roll and cut the top crust—any small shape, such as a tiny cookie cutter will work. And then place it on the pie and crimp.

Every January at the shop, we face our sad, wintry fate: any produce we're getting is coming straight from storage. What's a pie baker to do? The silver lining here is that one of our favorite farmers in Michigan grows the best sweet potatoes around. What's better yet is that both sweet potatoes and coconut are baking superstars, making for a smooth, hearty winter pie that is a lovely dessert accompaniment to a spicy chili or curry main course. You can just forget that sob story I started at the beginning of this paragraph. ❤

SWEET POTATO COCONUT PIE

Makes one 9-inch pie

FILLING

1 pound sweet potatoes

2 tablespoons (¼ stick) unsalted butter, melted and cooled

¾ cup packed light brown sugar

¼ teaspoon ground cardamom

½ teaspoon kosher salt

2 tablespoons fine yellow cornmeal

½ cup full-fat canned coconut milk

¼ cup heavy cream, at room temperature

6 large egg yolks, at room temperature

One 9-inch crust made with All-Butter Pie Dough (page 25), extra blind baked and cooled (page 50)

1 large egg, beaten

½ cup large flake coconut, toasted (see page 35)

First, roast the sweet potatoes: Preheat your oven to 425°F. Scrub the sweet potatoes and wrap them in aluminum foil. Poke a few holes through the foil and into the sweet potatoes with a fork, and transfer them to a baking sheet. Place the baking sheet in the oven and bake for 40 to 60 minutes, or until you can smoosh the foil package with your oven mitt. Remove from the oven and place on a wire rack. When cool enough to touch, carefully remove the skin from the sweet potatoes. Transfer the sweet potato flesh to a food processor or blender and puree until smooth. Set aside. This step can be done up to 2 days in advance. Store the sweet potato puree in an airtight container in the fridge.

Lower the oven temperature to 325°F. Line a baking sheet with parchment paper.

Make the filling: In a mixing bowl, combine the sweet potato puree with the butter, brown sugar, cardamom, salt, cornmeal, coconut milk, cream, and egg yolks and whisk until well blended.

Place the blind-baked shell on the parchment-lined baking sheet. Brush the crimped edge with the beaten egg. Pour the sweet potato filling into the pie shell until it reaches the bottom of the crimps. Transfer the baking sheet with the pie on it to the oven and bake for 40 to 50 minutes, until the edges are puffed and the center jiggles only slightly when shaken.

Remove the baking sheet from the oven and transfer the pie to a wire rack. Let cool for 15 minutes, then decorate the perimeter of the pie with the toasted coconut. Allow the pie to fully cool for another 4 to 6 hours. When the pie is at room temperature, slice it into 6 to 8 pieces and serve.

Store leftover pie, well wrapped in plastic wrap, in the refrigerator for up to 2 days.

ANYTIME
PIES

We embrace seasonal-pie baking with fervor (if you haven't already noticed). Even though Michigan is the second most agriculturally diverse state in the country, the winter season makes it challenging to feature local fruits and vegetables year round. In fact, we spend the cold months racking our brains for ideas about what sorts of pies we can prepare without produce, making it perhaps our most creative season. The pies you'll find in this chapter reflect what's listed on the Sister Pie chalkboard during various times throughout the calendar year. A few fruits (limes and lemons) are included in this chapter that aren't grown in Michigan, but we simply couldn't imagine our baking without them, so we cut ourselves some slack. You'll soon understand why.

The Salted Maple Pie is our signature flavor at Sister Pie because it is an homage to the bakeries where I got my professional chops: Momofuku Milk Bar in Manhattan and Four & Twenty Blackbirds in Brooklyn. It is reminiscent of the addictive quality of both Milk Bar's Crack Pie and Four & Twenty's Salty Honey Pie. We created our own version of a classic chess filling with robust Grade B maple syrup from Imlay City, Michigan and highlighted with local heavy cream, eggs, stone-ground yellow cornmeal, and light brown sugar. On Saturdays at the shop, we'll buy applewood-smoked bacon from the market to crisp up in the oven right before opening. It's a match made in pancake breakfast heaven. ♥

SALTED MAPLE PIE

Makes one 9-inch pie

FILLING

½ cup plus 2 tablespoons (1¼ sticks) unsalted butter, melted and cooled

1 cup Grade B maple syrup

¾ cup packed light brown sugar

¼ cup fine yellow cornmeal

Heaping ¼ teaspoon kosher salt

3 large eggs, at room temperature

1 large egg yolk, at room temperature

¾ cup heavy cream, at room temperature

1¼ teaspoons pure vanilla extract

One 9-inch crust made with All-Butter Pie Dough (page 25), blind baked and cooled (page 50)

1 large egg, beaten

Flaky sea salt, for sprinkling top

Preheat your oven to 350°F.

Make the filling: In a medium bowl, combine the melted butter and maple syrup. Whisk in the brown sugar, cornmeal, and kosher salt.

Crack the eggs and yolk into another medium bowl. Add the cream and vanilla and whisk until combined.

Slowly pour the egg mixture into the maple mixture and whisk just until combined.

Place the blind-baked shell on a parchment-lined baking sheet. Brush the crimped edge with the beaten egg. Pour the maple filling into the pie shell until it reaches the bottom of the crimps.

Transfer the baking sheet with the pie on it to the oven and bake for 45 minutes to 1 hour, until the edges are puffed and the center jiggles only slightly when shaken. It will continue to set as it cools.

Remove the baking sheet from the oven and transfer the pie to a wire rack to cool for 4 to 6 hours. Once fully cooled and at room temperature, sprinkle generously with flaky sea salt, slice into 6 to 8 pieces, and serve.

Store leftover pie, well wrapped in plastic wrap or under a pie dome, at room temperature for up to 3 days.

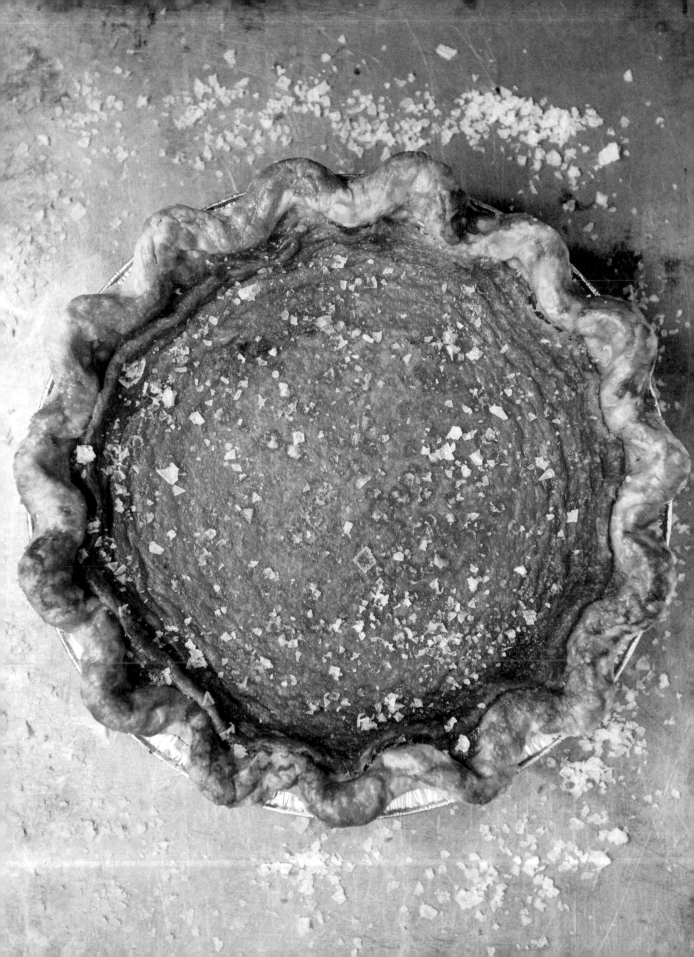

This recipe was inspired by a pie and coffee lover to the max: Special Agent Dale Cooper from David Lynch's cult masterpiece *Twin Peaks*. Sure, he's a fictional character, but the passion he exudes on-screen for that pie comes from a real place in his heart and stomach. This is simply a chess pie flavored with cold-brew coffee and espresso powder. Served with whipped cream, it's one delicious, caffeinated slice.

A note on the coffee: I tested this recipe with extra-strong coffee, cold brew, and espresso powder. The combination of cold brew and espresso powder won for its flavor punch of caffeinated mud, and while you might need to make a trip to the grocery store, I think you'll find it's worth it. ♥

COFFEE CHESS PIE

Makes one 9-inch pie

FILLING

1 cup packed light brown sugar

1 cup cold-brew coffee

½ cup (1 stick) unsalted butter, melted and cooled

2 tablespoons granulated sugar

¼ cup espresso powder

¼ cup fine yellow cornmeal

¼ teaspoon kosher salt

3 large eggs, at room temperature

1 cup heavy cream, at room temperature

1 tablespoon pure vanilla extract

One 9-inch crust made with All-Butter Pie Dough (page 25), extra blind baked and cooled (see page 50)

1 large egg, beaten

Preheat your oven to 325°F. Line a baking sheet with parchment paper.

Make the filling: In a saucepan over medium heat, whisk together the brown sugar and cold-brew coffee. Cook until the sugar has dissolved and the mixture has reduced by one-third, using a metal ruler or the handle of a wooden spoon as a gauge. Pour into a medium bowl and let cool slightly. You could make the coffee syrup up to 3 days in advance and store it in the refrigerator.

Whisk the melted butter, granulated sugar, espresso powder, cornmeal, and salt into the coffee mixture.

Crack the eggs into another medium bowl. Add the cream and vanilla and whisk until combined.

Slowly pour the egg mixture into the coffee mixture and whisk until combined.

Place the blind-baked shell on the parchment-lined baking sheet. Brush the crimped edge with the beaten egg. Pour the filling into the pie shell until it reaches the bottom of the crimps. Transfer the baking sheet with the pie on it to the oven and bake for 40 to 60 minutes, until the edges are puffed and the center jiggles only slightly when shaken. The filling will continue to set as it cools.

Remove the baking sheet from the oven and transfer the pie to a wire rack to cool for 4 to 6 hours. When the pie is at room temperature, slice it into 6 to 8 pieces and serve.

Store leftover pie, well wrapped in plastic wrap or under a pie dome, at room temperature for up to 3 days.

To envision this pie, first imagine a brownie that has coconut in it. Now imagine you've traveled back in time to before the brownie was actually a brownie. It was simply a gooey, rich chocolate batter flecked with thin shreds of sweetened coconut. And then think about how it would be to bake that brownie batter in a pie shell. Are you there yet?

Let me put it another way: This pie has the best parts of a brownie that are impossible to achieve at once—the shiny, crackling top and the raw, eggy batter. Through the magic of coconut milk, bittersweet chocolate, butter, and eggs, we've successfully combined the two, and added coconut because it makes most things more delicious.

Once baked and cooled, we top it with a small pool of ganache and toasted coconut chips. I highly recommend serving it warm with a big scoop of ice cream on top for the ultimate brownie sundae. ♥

CHOCOLATE COCONUT PIE

Makes one 9-inch pie

FILLING

1½ cups granulated sugar

1½ tablespoons fine yellow cornmeal

½ teaspoon kosher salt

¾ cup (1½ sticks) unsalted butter, cut into cubes

3 tablespoons bittersweet chocolate chips

3 tablespoons full-fat coconut milk

3 tablespoons cocoa powder

3 large eggs, at room temperature, lightly beaten

1¼ cups shredded, sweetened coconut

One 9-inch crust made with All-Butter Pie Dough (page 25), blind baked and cooled (page 50)

1 large egg, beaten

Preheat your oven to 350°F. Line a baking sheet with parchment paper.

Make the filling: Measure the sugar, cornmeal, and salt into a medium bowl.

In a saucepan over medium-low heat, melt the butter with the chocolate chips and coconut milk while stirring gently with a whisk to prevent scorching. Add the cocoa powder and stir until no clumps remain. Once the butter mixture is fully melted and incorporated, pour it over the sugar mixture. Whisk until completely mixed.

Slowly mix in the eggs until combined. Then, with a silicone spatula, gently fold in the shredded coconut.

Place the blind-baked shell on the parchment-lined baking sheet. Brush the crimped edge with the beaten egg. Pour the filling into the pie shell until it reaches the bottom of the crimps. Transfer the baking sheet with the pie on it to the oven and bake for 40 to 45 minutes, rotating the pie after 20 minutes. The pie will be very puffed in the middle. It will still jiggle quite a bit when shaken, but you can take it out once the middle of the pie has split away from the edge of the filling, which will have begun to crack.

GANACHE TOPPING

¼ cup heavy cream

2 ounces bittersweet chocolate, coarsely chopped

⅓ cup large flake coconut, toasted (see page 35)

Remove the baking sheet from the oven and transfer the pie to a wire rack to cool for 4 to 6 hours.

While the pie is cooling, make the ganache: In a small, heatproof bowl set over a pot of simmering water, combine the cream and chocolate pieces. Whisk until completely smooth. Remove from the heat and set aside to cool to room temperature. When the ganache and pie are both at room temperature, pour the ganache onto the center of the pie and spread it around with an offset spatula or the back of a spoon. Sprinkle the coconut flakes on top, slice into 6 to 8 pieces, and serve.

Store leftover pie, well wrapped in plastic wrap or under a pie dome, at room temperature for up to 2 days.

A NOTE ON COCONUT MILK

You might be annoyed that this recipe calls for you to open a can of coconut milk for a measly 3 tablespoons. Don't get mad, get creative! Use the extra coconut milk to make a batch of Coconut Drops (page 173) or a Sweet Potato Coconut Pie (page 105), or stir it into a soup for added creaminess.

We developed this pie because we wanted something hot pink on the menu for Valentine's Day. But whichever month you choose, it should please every single one of your pie lovers with its creamy, tart, and definitively earthy magenta filling, balanced out with brown butter. Even beet haters can get on board; tell them it's a red velvet pie and they'll be none the wiser. ♥

SWEET BEET PIE

Makes one 9-inch pie

FILLING

8 ounces whole red beets

6 tablespoons (¾ stick) unsalted butter

¾ cup packed light brown sugar

1½ tablespoons fine yellow cornmeal

¼ teaspoon kosher salt

3 large eggs, at room temperature

½ cup heavy cream, at room temperature

½ cup plain, thick yogurt (we use full-fat Greek-style yogurt), at room temperature

One 9-inch crust made with All-Butter Pie Dough (page 25), extra blind baked and cooled (page 50)

1 large egg, beaten

Make the filling: Preheat your oven to 425°F. Scrub the beets and trim off the ends. Wrap them tightly in aluminum foil and pierce through the foil into the beets with a fork a few times before placing in a baking dish or on a baking sheet. Roast for 40 to 50 minutes, until you can smoosh the foil package with your oven mitt. Remove the baking sheet from the oven and place on a wire rack. When cool enough to handle, open the foil package and carefully remove the skins from the beets. Transfer the beet flesh to a food processor or blender and puree until smooth. Set aside. You can roast the beets up to 2 days in advance and store the beet puree in an airtight container in the fridge.

Place the butter in a heavy-bottomed saucepan over medium heat, and use a silicone spatula to stir it gently occasionally. Swirl the pan every once in a while to distribute the heat evenly. You'll see the butter fully melt and separate, and then start to boil. It will typically go through two phases of boiling: first a clear, almost fluorescent, foam will form, followed by a soapy, white foam. Tiny brown specks will then appear, marking the first signs of the browning. Keep stirring, and do not leave unattended. The color will change from yellow to golden to a deep, toasted brown (similar to the color of beef stock or cola). If you're having trouble seeing the color beneath the foam, spoon a little into a clear glass and check. Set aside to cool slightly.

Preheat your oven to 325°F. Line a baking sheet with parchment paper.

CONTINUED

Complete the filling: In a medium bowl, combine the cooled browned butter with the beet puree, brown sugar, cornmeal, and salt and whisk until smooth.

Crack the eggs into another medium bowl. Add the cream and yogurt and whisk until combined.

Slowly pour the egg mixture into the beet mixture and whisk until combined and smooth.

Place the blind-baked shell on the parchment-lined baking sheet. Brush the crimped edge with the beaten egg. Pour the beet filling into the pie shell until it reaches the bottom of the crimps.

Transfer the baking sheet with the pie on it to the oven and bake the pie for 40 to 50 minutes, until the edges are just beginning to puff and the center jiggles only slightly when shaken. The filling will continue to set as it cools.

Remove the baking sheet from the oven and transfer the pie to a wire rack to cool completely, at least 4 hours. When the pie is at room temperature, slice it into 6 to 8 pieces and serve.

Store leftover pie in the refrigerator, well wrapped in plastic wrap, for up to 3 days.

This pie is a total powerhouse of citrus delight. It has been a regular on the Sister Pie menu since the beginning. It's one of my favorite recipes-in-progress to walk by at the bakery—the scent of lemon zest falling into sugar is intoxicating for a lemon lover like me. We balance the sugar with equal parts honey to create a smooth, sweet-tart flavor. The baked filling resembles lemon curd in texture and pairs perfectly with a big pile of cloud-like meringue. ♥

HONEY LEMON MERINGUE PIE

Makes one 9-inch pie

FILLING

¼ cup plus 2 tablespoons granulated sugar

Grated zest of 4 lemons

6 tablespoons (¾ stick) unsalted butter, melted and cooled

¼ cup plus 2 tablespoons mild-flavored honey (such as clover or orange blossom)

¼ cup plus 2 tablespoons fine yellow cornmeal

½ teaspoon kosher salt

4 large eggs, at room temperature

4 large egg yolks (reserve 3 whites for the meringue), at room temperature

¾ cup freshly squeezed lemon juice

1 cup heavy cream, at room temperature

One 9-inch crust made with All-Butter Pie Dough (page 25), extra blind baked and cooled (see page 50)

1 large egg, beaten

Preheat your oven to 325°F. Line a baking sheet with parchment paper.

First, make the filling: In a small bowl, combine ¼ cup of the granulated sugar and the lemon zest, rubbing them together with your fingertips until the mixture feels damp and slightly clumpy. Take a deep breath to inhale that sweet citrus scent. Set aside.

In a medium bowl, whisk the remaining 2 tablespoons sugar and the melted butter, honey, cornmeal, and salt until no big lumps remain. Stir in the sugar-zest mixture. Gently whisk in the eggs and egg yolks until smooth and just combined (whisking it for longer could incorporate excess air into the filling).

Slowly whisk the lemon juice into the honey-zest mixture, and then whisk in the cream. The mixture should be pale yellow and very smooth.

Place the blind-baked shell on the parchment-lined baking sheet. Brush the crimped edge with the beaten egg. Pour the honey-lemon filling into the pie shell until it reaches the bottom of the crimps. Transfer the baking sheet with the pie on it to the oven and bake for 40 to 50 minutes, until the edges are puffed and the center jiggles only slightly when shaken. It will continue to set as it cools.

Remove the pie from the oven and place on a cooling rack. Let the pie cool while you make the meringue.

CONTINUED

MERINGUE

6 large egg whites,
at room temperature

1 cup granulated sugar

¼ teaspoon cream of
tartar

¼ teaspoon kosher salt

Make the meringue: Whisk the egg whites, sugar, cream of tartar, and salt together in the bowl of a stand mixer set over a pan of simmering water until the sugar is completely dissolved. The mixture should be warm to the touch.

Transfer the bowl to the stand mixer fitted with the whisk attachment and whip on the highest speed until the egg whites are voluminous and shiny. To check for stiff peaks, stop the mixer and use a spatula or spoon to scoop up a tiny bit of the meringue. If the peak of the meringue stands tall on its own without falling over, your meringue is whipped enough. If not, continue to whip in the mixer until stiff peaks form.

Use a spatula to gently scrape all of the meringue onto the center of the cooled pie. Being careful not to deflate the meringue, spread it all the way to the crimps and finish it with whatever design you like. Use a kitchen torch to deeply toast the meringue. If you don't have a fancy kitchen torch, simply preheat your broiler or set the oven at 500°F and place the assembled pie back in the oven for 3 to 4 minutes. Be sure to watch the pie diligently—it can go from light brown to burnt in a matter of seconds.

Cool the pie completely, at least 4 to 6 hours, and then slice it into 6 to 8 pieces and serve.

Store leftover pie in the refrigerator under a pie dome for up to 3 days.

I'm a key lime pie fanatic. I love the creamy texture, the puckery-tart flavor, and the slightly savory graham crust. Our version is made with regular ol' limes, but there's nothing regular about it. We add malted milk powder and a pinch of cardamom to the filling, which we pour into a nontraditional all-butter crust. Don't worry—we haven't forgotten about the graham cracker element. Instead of store-bought graham crackers, we use actual graham flour to make a magical dust, lending that signature crunchy bite. If you can't find graham flour, substitute whole wheat flour.

This pie is best straight from the fridge, and it's essential to serve it with freshly whipped cream. ❤

MALTED LIME PIE

Makes one 9-inch pie

GRAHAM DUST

1 cup malted milk powder

½ cup graham flour

2 tablespoons tapioca starch

2 tablespoons granulated sugar

½ teaspoon kosher salt

¼ cup (½ stick) unsalted butter, melted

FILLING

Grated zest of 2 limes

5 large egg yolks, at room temperature

1 (14-ounce) can sweetened condensed milk (preferably organic)

¾ cup freshly squeezed lime juice (from 5 to 6 limes)

¼ teaspoon kosher salt

2 tablespoons malted milk powder

1 teaspoon ground cardamom

Make the Graham Dust: Preheat your oven to 325°F. Line a baking sheet with parchment paper. In a medium bowl, combine ½ cup of the malted milk powder and the graham flour, tapioca starch, sugar, and salt. Toss with your hands to mix. Add the melted butter and toss, using a silicone spatula, until the mixture starts to come together and form small clusters.

Spread the clusters onto the parchment-lined baking sheet and bake for 20 minutes. Remove the baking sheet from the oven and place it on a wire rack to fully cool. The mixture will have baked into one solid mass. Break into 1-inch pieces and place them back in the bowl. Combine with the remaining ½ cup malted milk powder, then transfer, 1 cup at a time, to a food processor and process until you have a fine graham crumb. Set aside while you make the filling. You can make the graham dust up to 3 days in advance and store in an airtight container in the refrigerator.

When you're ready to assemble the pie, preheat your oven to 300°F. Line the baking sheet with new parchment paper.

Make the filling: In a large bowl, whisk the lime zest, egg yolks, condensed milk, lime juice, salt, malted milk powder, and cardamom together until smooth.

One 9-inch crust made with All-Butter Pie Dough (page 25), extra blind baked 25 cooled (see page 50)

1 large egg, beaten

Whipped cream, for serving (see page 55)

Place the blind-baked shell on the parchment-lined baking sheet. Brush the crimped edge with the beaten egg. Pour the lime filling into the pie shell until it reaches the bottom of the crimps. Transfer the baking sheet with the pie on it to the oven and bake for 25 to 30 minutes, or until the pie begins to look set around the edges and tiny bubbles rise to the surface. Remove the baking sheet from the oven and place the pie on a cooling rack. Once the pie tin is cool enough to touch, transfer the pie to the refrigerator until fully set, about 1 hour.

Once the pie cooled and set, remove it from the fridge and cover the top with the Graham Dust. Slice the pie into 6 to 8 pieces, and serve with whipped cream.

Store leftover pie, well wrapped in plastic wrap, in the refrigerator for up to 3 days.

This pie is not for the faint of sweet. We dreamt it up in our early shop days in response to a butterscotch demand, and it has since evolved into our resplendent summer showpiece. The five components—an all-butter crust, a chocolate ganache layer, a butterscotch chess layer, and a homemade marshmallow creme that is then turned into a big pile of marshmallow meringue—make this one of our most laborious pies, but you'll feel absolutely like the queen of s'mores-like pies upon completion. ♥

TOASTED MARSHMALLOW BUTTERSCOTCH PIE

Makes one 9-inch pie

BITTERSWEET CHOCOLATE GANACHE

2 tablespoons heavy cream

2 ounces bittersweet chocolate chips

One 9-inch crust made with All-Butter Pie Dough (page 25), blind baked and cooled (page 50)

FILLING

½ cup (1 stick) unsalted butter, melted and cooled

1¼ cups packed dark brown sugar

¼ cup fine yellow cornmeal

½ teaspoon kosher salt

3 large eggs, at room temperature

1 large egg yolk, at room temperature (save the white for the marshmallow creme)

¼ cup whole milk, at room temperature

½ cup heavy cream, at room temperature

1 teaspoon pure vanilla extract

1 large egg, beaten

Make the ganache: In a heatproof bowl set over a saucepan of simmering water, combine the cream and chocolate chips. Stir with a silicone spatula until completely melted and smooth. Scrape into the blind-baked crust and allow to set while you prepare the filling. If your kitchen is warm, you could transfer the pie shell to the fridge or freezer until the ganache sets and is hard to the touch.

Preheat your oven to 350°F. Line a baking sheet with parchment paper.

Make the filling: In a medium bowl, combine the melted butter, brown sugar, cornmeal, and salt and whisk until combined and there are no cornmeal clumps.

In another medium bowl, combine the eggs, egg yolk, milk, cream, and vanilla. Slowly add the egg mixture to the butter mixture, whisking to combine as you pour.

Place the prepared pie shell on the parchment-lined baking sheet. Brush the crimps with the beaten egg. Pour the butterscotch filling into the pie shell. Transfer the baking sheet with the pie on it to the oven and bake for 50 to 60 minutes, until the edges have puffed and the center jiggles only slightly when shaken. Remove the baking sheet from the oven and transfer the pie to a cooling rack while you make the marshmallow meringue.

CONTINUED

MARSHMALLOW CREME

1 large egg white,
at room temperature

⅔ cup light corn syrup

¼ teaspoon kosher salt

⅔ cup powdered sugar

2 teaspoons pure vanilla
extract

**MARSHMALLOW
MERINGUE**

4 large egg whites,
at room temperature

½ cup granulated sugar

¼ teaspoon cream
of tartar

¼ teaspoon kosher salt

Handful of bittersweet
chocolate chips

Make the Marshmallow Creme: In the bowl of a stand mixer fitted with the whisk attachment, add the egg white, corn syrup, and salt. Mix on high speed for approximately 5 minutes, until the mixture is thick and almost doubled in volume. Reduce the speed to low, add the powdered sugar, and mix until well blended. Add the vanilla extract and mix until well blended. Scrape the mixture out of the bowl and set aside 1 cup for the meringue. The leftover creme can be used as a delicious dip for graham crackers or whatever your marshmallow-loving heart desires. Fully clean and dry the mixing bowl and whisk attachment before making the meringue.

Make the meringue: In a heatproof bowl set over a saucepan of simmering water, whisk the egg whites, sugar, cream of tartar, and salt until the sugar is completely dissolved. The mixture will be warm to the touch.

Transfer the mixture to a stand mixer fitted with a whisk attachment and whip on the highest speed until voluminous and shiny. To check for stiff peaks, stop the mixer and use a spatula or spoon to scoop up a tiny bit of the meringue. If the peak of the meringue stands tall on its own without falling over, your meringue is whipped enough. If not, continue to whip in the mixer until stiff peaks form.

Transfer the meringue to a medium bowl and add 1 cup Marshmallow Creme. Use a silicone spatula to gently fold the creme into the meringue.

Scrape all of the meringue onto the center of the cooled pie. Being careful not to deflate the meringue, spread it all the way up to the crimps and finish with whatever design you like. Use a kitchen torch to deeply toast the meringue. If you don't have a fancy kitchen torch, simply preheat your broiler or set the oven at 500°F and place the assembled pie back in the oven for 3 to 4 minutes. Be sure to check the pie diligently—it can go from light brown to burnt in a matter of seconds.

Decorate the top with the bittersweet chocolate chips, following your swirls in the meringue.

Cool the pie completely, at least 4 hours, then slice into 6 to 8 pieces and serve.

Store leftover pie at room temperature for up to 3 days.

Throughout most of my childhood, I lived across the street from two girls named Katie and Kristen. Their mother, Tresa, was an incredible cook, and her specialty was a rich, mega-savory steak and potato pie. It blew my young mind right open, with its tender pieces of red meat, creamy potatoes, thick, buttery crust, and a scattering of big salt flakes on top.

What began as a large-format savory, meaty pie memory turned into vegetable-stuffed pocket-size hand pies—a breeze to assemble and perfect for selling at farmers' markets and wholesale accounts in Detroit. Our flavors change on a weekly basis, depending entirely on what our farmers bring us. It's the kind of constant creative challenge that gets us out of bed every day.

In this chapter, you'll find recipes for four savory hand pies plus one sweet version to make throughout the year. But remember, you can put almost anything inside a hand pie: leftover dinner scraps smooshed together, extra pie filling, jam, nut butters, and more.

As for the other pies in this book, we refer you to the relevant pages from The Dough and The Crust when making hand pies. My preferred game plan is to make the dough and the filling on day one, then assemble and bake on day two.

Delicata squash became my top pick for autumnal squash when I learned that no peeling was necessary. Not only did this revelation eliminate my least favorite squash preparation step, but leaving the squash skin on adds a textural element that takes roasted squash from soup-root to snack-root. You'll especially appreciate that texture variance alongside the otherwise creamy filling. These are best served warm, alongside a big arugula salad. ♥

CARAMELIZED ONION, DELICATA SQUASH, AND SAGE HAND PIES

Makes 10 hand pies

FILLING

1½ pounds delicata squash, halved lengthwise, seeded, and cut into ½-inch cubes

2 tablespoons olive oil

¾ teaspoon kosher salt, plus more as needed

4 yellow onions, thinly sliced lengthwise

1 tablespoon light brown sugar

Splash of apple cider vinegar (optional)

⅓ cup minced fresh sage leaves

4 ounces goat cheese, crumbled

Freshly ground black pepper

All-Butter Hand Pie Dough (page 27), rolled into 20 (4-inch) rounds, laid on a parchment-lined baking sheet, wrapped in plastic wrap, and refrigerated

1 large egg, beaten

2 teaspoons poppy seeds

½ teaspoon flaky sea salt

Make the filling: Preheat your oven to 400°F. Place the cubed squash on a baking sheet and toss evenly with 1 tablespoon of the olive oil and ¼ teaspoon of the salt. Transfer the baking sheet to the oven and roast for 40 to 50 minutes, or until the squash is fork-tender and caramelized. Remove the baking sheet from the oven and set on a cooling rack. You can roast the squash up to 2 days in advance and store it in the refrigerator in an airtight container.

Meanwhile, heat the remaining 1 tablespoon olive oil in a large skillet over medium heat. Stir in the onions and brown sugar. Decrease the heat to medium-low and cook, stirring often, until the onions begin to turn golden. After about 10 minutes, add the remaining ½ teaspoon salt and continue to cook until the onions are deep brown and texturally jammy, at least another 10 minutes. If the pan has lots of onion stuck to it, add a splash of apple cider vinegar and use your spatula to scrape them up as the vinegar sizzles and releases what's stuck. You can caramelize the onions up to 2 days in advance and store them in an airtight container in the refrigerator.

In a large bowl, combine the squash and onions with the sage and goat cheese. Use your hands or a wooden spoon to mix them together—the goat cheese will soften slightly as you mix, acting as a binder. Taste and adjust the seasoning with more salt and pepper. Cover with plastic wrap and transfer to the refrigerator to cool. You can make the filling up to 2 days in advance and store in an airtight container in the refrigerator until you're ready to assemble the hand pies.

CONTINUED

Preheat the oven to 450°F. Line two baking sheets with parchment paper.

Remove the rolled-out pie crust rounds from the refrigerator and lay half of them out on a lightly floured surface. Brush each round entirely with the beaten egg. Spoon 2 to 3 tablespoons of the squash filling onto the center of each round. Place the remaining pie crust rounds on top of each pile of filling. Place your fingers under either side of a hand pie while resting your thumbs on the top. Use your thumbs to press the edges of the bottom round up to meet the top round and pinch them together tightly until the hand pie is sealed, rotating the pie as you go. Flip the hand pie over and use the tines of a fork (dipped in flour) to seal it again around the edge of the entire round, making a decorative edge. Take a 4-inch cutter and cut the hand pie once more to clean and define the edges. Repeat with the remaining hand pies. If you want to freeze the hand pies to bake them later, do that now: transfer them to a baking sheet and place in the freezer. When frozen, place in a freezer storage bag and freeze for up to 3 months. Transfer from the freezer directly to the oven to bake.

Divide the hand pies between the parchment-lined baking sheets, placing them at least ½ inch apart. Use a paring knife to cut a tiny slit in the top of each hand pie, then brush the tops and edges with the remaining beaten egg. Sprinkle the poppy seeds and sea salt evenly on the tops.

Transfer the baking sheets to the oven and bake for 25 to 35 minutes, until the hand pies are deeply golden brown. Place on a wire rack and let cool for at least 10 minutes before eating.

Store leftover hand pies, in an airtight container or wrapped tightly in plastic wrap or foil, in the refrigerator for up to 2 days.

If there were a hand pie fan club, this is the hand pie they'd serve at their meetings. It's got every element of a great stuffed pocket: potato, beans, and cheese! When we don't have it for sale at the shop, we hear about it.

We use organic dried beans for any dish that calls for them at Sister Pie—mostly salads, soups, and hand pies. Although dried beans typically yield a more flavorful result, opting for the quicker, canned bean route is A-okay in our book . . . this book! For instructions on how to cook dried beans, see page 12. ♥

SWEET POTATO, BLACK BEAN, AND FETA HAND PIES

Makes 10 hand pies

FILLING

1 pound sweet potatoes, scrubbed and chopped into ½-inch cubes

1 tablespoon olive oil

½ teaspoon kosher salt, plus more as needed

¾ teaspoon ground cumin

1 (15-ounce) can black beans, drained

4 ounces feta cheese, crumbled

3 scallions, white and green parts, rinsed clean and sliced

Freshly ground black pepper

All-Butter Hand Pie Dough (page 27), rolled into 20 (4-inch) rounds, on a parchment-lined baking sheet, wrapped in plastic wrap, and refrigerated

1 large egg, beaten

¼ teaspoon ground cumin

½ teaspoon flaky sea salt

Make the filling: Preheat your oven to 400°F. Place the sweet potatoes on a baking sheet and toss evenly with the olive oil, salt, and cumin. Transfer to the oven and roast for 40 to 50 minutes, until the sweet potatoes are fork-tender and caramelized. Set on a wire rack to cool. You can roast the sweet potatoes up to 2 days in advance and store them in an airtight container in the refrigerator.

In a medium mixing bowl, combine the black beans, feta, scallions, and slightly cooled sweet potatoes. Use your hands or a wooden spoon to mix together—we like to smash the sweet potatoes so they become the binder. Season the mixture with more salt and the pepper. Cover with plastic wrap and transfer to the refrigerator to cool. You can make the filling up to 2 days in advance and store in an airtight container in the refrigerator until you're ready to assemble the hand pies.

Preheat the oven to 450°F. Line two baking sheets with parchment paper.

Remove the rolled-out pie crust rounds from the refrigerator and lay half of them out onto a lightly floured surface. Brush each round entirely with the beaten egg. Spoon 2 to 3 tablespoons of the sweet potato filling onto the center of each round. Place the remaining pie crust rounds on top of each pile of filling. Place your fingers under either side of a hand pie while resting your thumbs on the top. Use your thumbs to press the edges of the bottom round up to meet the top round and pinch them together tightly until the hand pie is sealed, rotating the pie as you go. Flip the hand pie over and use the tines of a fork (dipped in flour) to seal it again around the edge of the entire round, making a decorative edge. Take a 4-inch cutter and cut the hand pie once more to clean and define the edges. Repeat with the remaining hand pies. If you want to freeze the hand pies to bake later, do that now: transfer them to a baking sheet and place in the freezer. When frozen, place in a freezer storage bag and freeze for up to 3 months. Transfer from the freezer directly to the oven to bake.

Divide the hand pies between the parchment-lined baking sheets, placing them at least ½ inch apart. Use a paring knife to cut a tiny slit in the top of each hand pie, then brush the tops and edges with the remaining beaten egg. Mix the cumin with the sea salt in a little bowl, then sprinkle evenly on the tops. Transfer the baking sheets to the oven and bake for 25 to 35 minutes, until the hand pies are deeply golden brown. Place on a rack to cool for at least 10 minutes before eating.

Store leftover hand pies, in an airtight container or wrapped tightly in plastic wrap or foil, in the refrigerator for up to 2 days.

It's like a coming-of-vegetable-age story when you try fresh peas for the first time. A food I was sure I hated from the can turned into something I'm dying to see at the market. These hand pies are a celebration of peas, with fresh mint and lemon to provide brightness and roasted, mashed potatoes to bring it all together (literally and figuratively). Dip them in extra sour cream for a real treat. ♥

MINTED PEA AND POTATO HAND PIES

Makes 10 hand pies

FILLING

8 ounces red-skinned potatoes (skin on), scrubbed and chopped into ½-inch cubes

2 tablespoons olive oil

1 teaspoon kosher salt, plus more as needed

1¼ teaspoons freshly ground black pepper, plus more as needed

1 tablespoon unsalted butter

1 large yellow onion, diced

2 cloves garlic, minced

2 scallions, white and green parts, rinsed clean and sliced

1 teaspoon packed grated lemon zest

1½ cups fresh shelled peas (frozen works, too)

⅓ cup minced fresh mint leaves

½ cup sour cream or thick plain yogurt

All-Butter Hand Pie Dough (page 27), rolled into 20 (4-inch) rounds, on a parchment-lined baking sheet, wrapped in plastic wrap, and refrigerated

1 large egg, beaten

½ teaspoon flaky sea salt

Make the filling: Preheat your oven to 400°F. Place the potatoes on a baking sheet and toss evenly with 1 tablespoon of the olive oil, ½ teaspoon of the salt, and 1 teaspoon of the pepper. Transfer the baking sheet to the oven and roast for 40 to 50 minutes, until the potatoes are fork-tender and beginning to look crispy. Set the baking sheet on a wire rack to cool. You can roast the potatoes up to 2 days in advance and store in an airtight container in the refrigerator.

In a large sauté pan over medium heat, melt the butter and remaining 1 tablespoon olive oil. Add the onion and cook, stirring occasionally, until translucent. Add the garlic, scallions, and lemon zest and cook for 1 minute longer. Season with the remaining ½ teaspoon salt and ¼ teaspoon pepper. Add the peas all at once, and stir to mix. Cook for 5 minutes, until the peas turn very bright green. Add the mint and cook for 1 more minute. You can cook the peas up to 2 days in advance and store in an airtight container in the refrigerator.

In a large bowl, combine the potatoes, pea mixture, and sour cream. Use your hands or a wooden spoon to mix together—we like to smash the potatoes so they become the binder. Season to taste with more salt and pepper. Cover with plastic wrap and transfer to the refrigerator to cool. You can make the filling up to 2 days in advance and store in an airtight container in the refrigerator until you're ready to assemble the hand pies.

Preheat the oven to 450°F. Line two baking sheets with parchment paper.

CONTINUED

Remove the rolled-out pie crust rounds from the refrigerator and lay half of them out onto a lightly floured surface. Brush each round entirely with the beaten egg. Spoon 2 to 3 tablespoons of the pea filling onto the center of each round. Place the remaining pie crust rounds on top of each pile of filling. Place your fingers under either side of a hand pie while resting your thumbs on the top. Use your thumbs to press the edges of the bottom round up to meet the top round and pinch them together tightly until the hand pie is sealed, rotating the pie as you go. Flip the hand pie over and use the tines of a fork (dipped in flour) to seal it again around the edge of the entire round, making a decorative edge. Take a 4-inch cutter and cut the hand pie once more to clean and define the edges. Repeat with the remaining hand pies. If you want to freeze the hand pies to bake later, do that now: transfer them to a baking sheet and place in the freezer. When frozen, place in a freezer storage bag and freeze for up to 3 months. Transfer from the freezer directly to the oven to bake.

Divide the hand pies between the parchment-lined baking sheets, placing them at least ½ inch apart. Use a paring knife to cut a tiny slit in the top of each hand pie, then brush the tops and edges with the remaining beaten egg. Sprinkle the sea salt evenly on the tops. Transfer the baking sheets to the oven and bake for 25 to 35 minutes, until the hand pies are deeply golden brown. Place on a rack to cool at least 10 minutes before eating.

Store leftover hand pies, in an airtight container or wrapped tightly in plastic wrap or foil, in the refrigerator for up to 2 days.

Also known as "pizza pies," these hand pies are perfectly adaptable to include whatever you like on your slice. Swap out the olives for diced green peppers and you'll have my mom and dad's pizza order in hand pie form. Ditch the fresh tomato for slices of pepperoni topped with your favorite tomato sauce. A dollop of ricotta with a pile of caramelized red onions is divine. Ham and pineapple your thing? Nobody's gonna stop your magic. Everything from the sesame-topped crust to the dip in cornmeal makes this the pizza-pie hybrid the world's been asking for. ♥

TOMATO, OLIVE, AND MOZZARELLA HAND PIES

Makes 10 hand pies

FILLING

2 tablespoons olive oil

⅔ cup minced shallots (from 1 or 2 shallots)

6 cloves garlic, minced

⅔ cup finely chopped kalamata or Castelvetrano olives

3 tablespoons minced fresh oregano leaves

½ teaspoon kosher salt

⅛ teaspoon crushed red pepper flakes

All-Butter Hand Pie Dough (page 27), rolled into 20 (4-inch rounds), on a parchment-lined baking sheet, wrapped in plastic wrap, and refrigerated

2 large eggs, beaten

3 to 4 small tomatoes on the vine, cut into ¼-inch-thick slices

8 ounces fresh mozzarella, cut into slices ¼ inch thick and 1½ to 2 inches wide

½ cup fine yellow cornmeal

½ teaspoon flaky sea salt

1 teaspoon sesame seeds

Make the filling: Heat the olive oil in a medium skillet over medium heat. Add the shallots and cook, stirring occasionally, until translucent. Add the garlic, olives, oregano, salt, and red pepper flakes and cook for 1 minute longer. Remove from the heat and set aside to cool. You can cook this mixture up to 2 days in advance and store in an airtight container in the refrigerator until you're ready to assemble the hand pies.

Preheat the oven to 450°F. Line two baking sheets with parchment paper.

Remove the rolled-out pie crust rounds from the refrigerator and lay half of them out onto a lightly floured surface. Brush each round entirely with the beaten egg. Place a tomato slice on each round. Divide the shallot mixture among the rounds. Top each with a mozzarella slice. Place the remaining pie crust rounds on top of each pile of filling. Place your fingers under either side of a hand pie while resting your thumbs on the top. Use your thumbs to press the edges of the bottom round up to meet the top round and pinch them together tightly until the hand pie is sealed, rotating the pie as you go. Flip the hand pie over and use the tines of a fork (dipped in flour) to seal it again around the edge of the entire round, making a decorative edge. Take a 4-inch cutter and cut the hand pie once more to clean and define the edges. Repeat with the remaining hand pies. If you want to freeze the hand pies to bake later, do that now: transfer them to a baking sheet and

CONTINUED

place in the freezer. When frozen, place in a freezer storage bag and freeze for up to 3 months. Transfer from the freezer directly to the oven to bake.

Place the ½ cup cornmeal in a cereal bowl. Brush the bottom of each hand pie with egg wash and dip into the cornmeal, then place on the baking sheets, at least ½ inch apart. Use a paring knife to cut a tiny slit in the top of each hand pie, then brush the tops and edges with the remaining beaten egg. Sprinkle the sea salt and sesame seeds evenly on top.

Transfer the baking sheets to the oven and bake for 25 to 35 minutes, until the hand pies are deeply golden brown. Place on a wire rack and let cool for at least 10 minutes before eating. Eat them while they're still warm for gooey mozzarella goodness.

Store leftover hand pies, in an airtight container or wrapped tightly in plastic wrap or foil, in the refrigerator for up to 2 days.

HAND PIE MAKE-AHEAD

You can assemble the hand pies in advance and freeze them for up to three months before baking. To do so, simply place the unbaked hand pies on a parchment-lined baking sheet and transfer to your freezer for at least 1 hour. Once the hand pies are frozen solid, stack them together and wrap tightly in plastic wrap. Follow the directions for baking below, keeping in mind that you might need to add a few minutes to the final bake time.

This flavor is a Sister Pie classic—the first example of my obsession with alternative crusts. We use organic dark rye flour from our favorite local mill. The flour speckles the dough in shades of chestnut. The sharp white Cheddar cheese complements the sweet-tart flavor of Michigan apples. ♥

APPLE CHEDDAR RYE HAND PIES

Makes 10 hand pies

FILLING

2 Northern Spy, Idared, or Golden Delicious apples, peeled and sliced

½ teaspoon freshly squeezed lemon juice

¼ cup granulated sugar

2 tablespoons packed light brown sugar

2 tablespoons tapioca starch

⅛ teaspoon ground cinnamon

⅛ teaspoon ground nutmeg

¼ teaspoon kosher salt

Cheddar Rye Hand Pie Dough (page 37), rolled into 20 (4-inch) rounds, laid on a parchment-lined baking sheet, wrapped in plastic wrap, and refrigerated

1 large egg, beaten

2 tablespoons Sugar-Sugar (see page 12)

Make the filling: Place the apples in a large bowl and toss with the lemon juice. In a small bowl, combine the granulated and brown sugars, tapioca starch, cinnamon, nutmeg, and salt. Pour over the apples and toss with your hands until evenly distributed.

Preheat the oven to 450°F. Line two baking sheets with parchment paper.

Remove the rolled-out pie crust rounds from the refrigerator and lay half of them out onto a lightly floured surface. Brush each round entirely with the beaten egg. Arrange 4 to 5 slices of apples on each round, core side down, leaving at least a ½-inch border. Place the remaining pie crust rounds on top of each pile of filling. Place your fingers under either side of a hand pie while resting your thumbs on the top. Use your thumbs to press the edges of the bottom round up to meet the top round and pinch them together tightly until the hand pie is sealed. Flip the hand pie over and use the tines of a fork (dipped in flour) to seal it again around the edge of the entire round, making a decorative edge. Take a 4-inch cutter and cut the hand pie once more to clean and define the edges. Repeat with the remaining hand pies. If you want to freeze the hand pies to bake later, do that now: transfer them to a baking sheet and place in the freezer. When frozen, place in a freezer storage bag and freeze for up to 3 months. Transfer from the freezer directly to the oven to bake.

Divide the hand pies between the parchment-lined baking sheets, placing them at least ½ inch apart. Use a paring knife to cut a tiny slit in the top of each hand pie, then brush the tops and edges with the remaining beaten egg. Sprinkle the Sugar-Sugar evenly on top.

Transfer the baking sheets to the oven and bake for 25 to 35 minutes, until the hand pies are deeply golden brown. Place on a wire rack and let cool for at least 10 minutes before eating.

Store leftover hand pies in an airtight container at room temperature for up to 2 days.

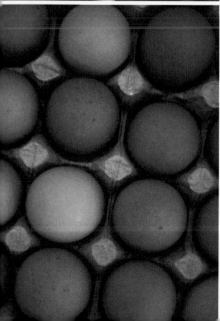

AND EVERYTHING ELSE

While we have committed ourselves to a bakery menu that (often rapidly) changes with the seasons, we cannot deny that people crave consistency. Thank goodness for shortbread, cookies, and bars! Our pastry case selection reflects an abundance of our favorite ingredients to make our non-pie sweet options both complex and approachable. In this chapter, you'll find everything from a vegan, gluten-free brownie to a savory-sweet rosemary shortbread to a pretzel-studded cookie named after a classic movie star. Might I suggest starting a cookie-baking club in your neighborhood? But first, some tips for success.

What's room-temperature butter, anyway?:
Long gone are the days when we believed
that super-soft butter was what should be
mixed into cookie dough. If the butter is too
warm, the process of creaming is for naught.
Allowing your butter to rest for an hour or so
out of the fridge should do the trick. Ideally,
butter should not be warmer than 70°F
before creaming.

Cream machine: Pay close attention to the
creaming instructions in the cookie recipes.
For shortbreads, we cream only until the
ingredients are smooth. This results in a
tender, crumbly, traditional shortbread. For
scooped cookies, we cream the heck out of
the butter and sugar for at least 4 minutes.
This process incorporates ample air into the
ingredients, resulting in a lighter cookie.

Cool sheets: If you have one baking sheet
and are baking multiple sets of cookies, be
sure to cool down the sheet between bakes.
Putting the dough onto a warm sheet will
result in unevenly baked cookies that spread
far too much during baking.

Dough rest: We rest all of our shortbread
and cookie doughs (with one exception,
on page 168) overnight in the fridge. This
process (and patience!) allows flavors to
deepen and prevents the cookie from
spreading too much while baking. Remove
the dough from your fridge a couple hours
before you intend to scoop it, depending
on how warm your kitchen is.

Shape up!: Several of the cookie doughs
in this chapter get shaped into logs before
being chilled, sliced, and baked. See how
we roll those logs on page 154.

One of the first weddings that featured Sister Pie desserts was at a nearby, much-loved Detroit park called Belle Isle. The bride, Sandra, had a vision for a dessert table filled with various platters piled high with cookies. To quote Ina Garten, "How bad can that be?"

Sandra selected from our small but developing cookie menu and had a few ideas of her own. She raved about a latte she once tried that featured fresh rosemary and sea salt, and wondered if that combination could be magically transformed into a shortbread. It sounded simple enough to me, and simple it stayed: this cookie is pure butter and rosemary. ♥

SALTED ROSEMARY SHORTBREAD

Makes 30 cookies

2 cups all-purpose flour

½ teaspoon kosher salt

1 cup (2 sticks) unsalted butter, at room temperature

½ cup powdered sugar

2 tablespoons finely minced fresh rosemary

Flaky sea salt, for sprinkling tops

In a medium bowl, whisk together the flour and kosher salt. Set aside.

Place the butter, powdered sugar, and rosemary in the bowl of a stand mixer fitted with the paddle attachment and cream on medium speed for about 3 minutes, until very smooth with no visible chunks of butter.

Use a silicone spatula to scrape down the bowl, then add the flour and salt mixture and mix until just combined. Remove the dough from the bowl and shape into a square pack, about ½ inch thick. Wrap in plastic wrap and refrigerate for 40 minutes. You can mix the dough up to 2 days in advance and store it in the refrigerator until 1 hour before you intend to roll out the dough. Alternatively, you may freeze the dough for up to 3 months, then let it thaw in the refrigerator overnight before proceeding with the recipe.

Preheat your oven to 350°F. Line two baking sheets with parchment paper.

Remove the dough from the refrigerator, unwrap it, and place on a lightly floured surface. Use a rolling pin to roll the dough to ¼-inch thickness. Cut out 2-inch shapes with your favorite cookie cutter and carefully transfer them to the parchment-lined baking sheets. Gather the scraps and form into another ½-inch-thick square, then

reroll and cut more cookies. Repeat until you have no scraps left. Top each shortbread with a few flakes of sea salt.

Place the baking sheets in the oven and bake for 16 to 18 minutes, until the edges are just slightly golden.

Remove the baking sheets from the oven and transfer the cookies to wire racks to cool completely. Store in an airtight container at room temperature for up to 1 week.

DIAMONDS IN OUR EYES

We stamp our shortbread cookies out with a 2-inch fluted square cutter, and we use a tiny diamond cutter to cut a shape from the center. You can bake the tiny diamonds on a separate baking sheet, as they will not need as much oven time. This is a pretty specific look and has almost zero effect on how delicious the cookies taste. Feel free to use the cookie cutter of your choice. Keep in mind that using a cutter that is larger or smaller than 2 inches will change the yield, and you'll also likely need to adjust the baking time by 1 to 3 minutes.

These cookies are a heavenly delight and one of my favorite shortbreads at Sister Pie. They're light and buttery, as any good shortbread should be, with an added deep, toasted flavor from the dark rye flour. The kick of ginger spice and the chewy candied ginger chunks are exactly what will keep you coming back for more. ♥

GINGER RYE SHORTBREAD

Makes 30 cookies

1 cup all-purpose flour

1 cup dark rye flour

½ teaspoon kosher salt

1 teaspoon ground ginger

1 cup (2 sticks) unsalted butter, at room temperature

¼ cup packed light brown sugar

¼ cup powdered sugar

½ teaspoon pure vanilla extract

½ cup finely chopped candied ginger

Turbinado sugar, for sprinkling tops

In a medium bowl, whisk together the all-purpose flour and rye flour, salt, and ground ginger. Set aside.

Place the butter, brown sugar, and powdered sugar in the bowl of a stand mixer fitted with the paddle attachment and cream on medium speed for about 3 minutes, until very smooth with no visible chunks of butter. Add the vanilla and mix until just combined.

Use a silicone spatula to scrape down the bowl, then add the flour mixture and mix until almost fully incorporated—you should still be able to see some streaks of flour. Add the candied ginger and mix until just combined. Remove the dough from the bowl and shape into a square pack, about ½ inch thick. Wrap in plastic wrap and refrigerate for 40 minutes. You can mix the dough up to 2 days in advance and store it in the refrigerator until 1 hour before you intend to roll out the dough. Alternatively, you may freeze the dough for up to 3 months, then let it thaw in the refrigerator overnight before proceeding with the recipe.

Preheat your oven to 350°F. Line two baking sheets with parchment paper.

Remove the dough from the refrigerator, unwrap it, and place on a lightly floured surface. Use a rolling pin to roll the dough to ¼-inch thickness. Cut out 2-inch shapes with your favorite cookie cutter and carefully transfer to the parchment-lined baking sheets. Gather the scraps and form into another ½-inch-thick square, then reroll and cut more cookies. Repeat until you have no scraps left. Top each shortbread with a pinch of turbinado sugar.

Place the baking sheets in the oven and bake for 16 to 18 minutes, until the edges are just slightly golden.

Remove the baking sheets from the oven and transfer the cookies to wire racks to cool completely. Store in an airtight container at room temperature for up to 1 week.

ROUNDERS

For our version of these cookies at the shop, we use a 2-inch round cutter. Feel free to use the cookie cutter of your choice. Keep in mind that using a cutter that is larger or smaller than 2 inches will change the yield, and you'll also likely need to adjust the baking time by 1 to 3 minutes.

These cookies are floral and delicate, laced with salty pistachios and edible, fragrant rose petals—a classic Middle Eastern flavor combination. After they're baked and cooled, we spread a thin layer of creamy Rose Petal Icing on top. They remind me of eating a scoop of Kashta Pistachio ice at my favorite dessert emporium in Dearborn, and also of chowing down on iced animal cookies as an eight-year-old in Milford. ♥

ROSE PISTACHIO SHORTBREAD

Makes 30 cookies

SHORTBREAD DOUGH

2 cups all-purpose flour

¼ cup roasted and salted pistachios, finely chopped

½ teaspoon kosher salt

1 cup (2 sticks) unsalted butter, at room temperature

¾ cup powdered sugar

2 tablespoons crushed, dried, edible rose petals

½ teaspoon rose flower water

ROSE PETAL ICING

¾ cup powdered sugar, plus more as needed

⅛ teaspoon rose flower water

½ teaspoon coconut oil, melted

3 tablespoons heavy cream, plus more as needed

⅛ teaspoon kosher salt

1½ teaspoons crushed, dried, edible rose petals

Mix the dough: In a medium bowl, whisk together the flour, pistachios, and salt. Set aside.

Place the butter, powdered sugar, and rose petals in the bowl of a stand mixer fitted with the paddle attachment and cream on medium speed for about 3 minutes, until very smooth with no visible chunks of butter.

Use a silicone spatula to scrape down the bowl, then add the rose flower water and mix until just incorporated. Add the flour mixture and mix until completely incorporated. Remove the dough from the bowl and shape into a square log approximately 1¾ inches in diameter (see page 154). Wrap tightly in plastic wrap and refrigerate for at least 40 minutes. You can mix and shape the dough up to 2 days in advance and store it in the refrigerator until 1 hour before you intend to roll out the dough. Alternatively, you may freeze the dough for up to 3 months, then let it thaw in the refrigerator overnight before proceeding with the recipe.

Preheat your oven to 350°F. Line two baking sheets with parchment paper.

Remove the dough from the refrigerator, unwrap it, and place on a cutting board. Using a sharp chef's knife, slice the cookies about ¼ inch thick. Carefully transfer them to the parchment-lined baking sheets.

Place the baking sheets in the oven and bake for 16 to 18 minutes, until the edges are just slightly golden.

CONTINUED

Remove the baking sheets from the oven and transfer the cookies to wire racks to cool.

Make the icing: While the cookies are cooling, in a medium bowl whisk together the powdered sugar, rose flower water, coconut oil, cream, and salt until very smooth. The texture should remind you of Elmer's glue. Yum! If the icing it seems a little dry, whisk in a small splash of heavy cream. If it seems too wet, whisk in powdered sugar, 1 tablespoon at a time. Stir in the rose petals.

Once the cookies have fully cooled, use a small offset spatula or knife to spread a very thin, even layer of icing across the tops of the cookies. It should be carefully smoothed, not gloppy. Return the cookies to the baking sheets to give the icing a chance to set up before serving. Store the iced cookies in an airtight container for up to 1 week.

These are the lime-flavored, grown-up version of one of my favorite childhood grocery store cookies—the lemon cooler. These buttery, light, citrus-packed cookies are coated in powdered sugar that gets everywhere with each bite. I've re-created the classic as a more traditional shortbread (read: more butter) with plenty of lime zest and fresh mint. The kid in me is pretty happy with the result. ♥

FRESH MINT AND LIME SHORTBREAD

Makes 36 cookies

2¼ cups all-purpose flour

½ teaspoon kosher salt

¼ cup finely minced fresh mint leaves

1 teaspoon granulated sugar

1 cup (2 sticks) unsalted butter, at room temperature

¾ cup powdered sugar, plus more for coating

2 teaspoons packed grated lime zest

3 tablespoons freshly squeezed lime juice

In a medium bowl, whisk together the flour and salt. Set aside. In another small bowl, massage the mint with the granulated sugar.

Place the butter, powdered sugar, lime zest, and mint mixture in the bowl of a stand mixer fitted with the paddle attachment and cream on medium speed for about 3 minutes, or until very smooth with no visible chunks of butter.

Use a silicone spatula to scrape down the bowl, then add the lime juice and mix until just incorporated. Add the flour and salt all at once and mix on low speed until completely incorporated. Remove the dough from the bowl and shape into a cylindrical log approximately 1½ inches in diameter (see opposite). Wrap tightly in plastic wrap and refrigerate for at least 40 minutes. You can mix and shape the dough up to 2 days in advance and store it in the refrigerator until 1 hour before you intend to roll out the dough. Alternatively, you may freeze the dough for up to 3 months, then let it thaw in the refrigerator overnight before proceeding with the recipe.

Preheat your oven to 350°F. Line two baking sheets with parchment paper.

Remove the dough from the refrigerator, unwrap it, and place on a cutting board. Using a sharp chef's knife, slice the cookies about ¼ inch thick. Carefully transfer them to the parchment-lined baking sheet.

Place the baking sheets in the oven and bake for 14 to 16 minutes, until the edges are just slightly golden.

Remove the baking sheets from the oven and transfer the cookies to wire racks to cool completely. Before serving, toss the cookies in additional powdered sugar. Store in an airtight container for up to 1 week.

Every year for the holidays, we sell a shortbread trio—a pound of cookies all wrapped up in red yarn and ready to give to the butter lover in your life. One season we were particularly inspired by cocktails. Upon discovering that gin was made from juniper berries, I experimented with using them in a savory-sweet cookie. With bright green, briny Castelvetrano olives and freshly crushed juniper berries, this shortbread is an homage to the classic gin martini, minus the vermouth (but not the fun). ♥

JUNIPER OLIVE SHORTBREAD

Makes 36 cookies

2 cups all-purpose flour

½ teaspoon kosher salt

1 cup (2 sticks) unsalted butter, at room temperature

¾ cup powdered sugar

1 tablespoon crushed juniper berries

5 tablespoons finely chopped Castelvetrano olives, squeezed gently to remove excess liquid

---

JUMPING JUNIPER (BERRIES)!

You should be able to find juniper berries in the spice aisle of your favorite grocery store or easily online. To crush them for this recipe, place them between 2 sheets of parchment in a deep, wide metal bowl, or inside a plastic bag, and use a kitchen mallet or the bottom of a metal measuring cup to bust them open. Alternatively, you could pulse them in a spice grinder just until they're in fragments (not finely ground).

In a medium bowl, whisk together the flour and salt. Set aside.

Place the butter, powdered sugar, and juniper in the bowl of a stand mixer fitted with the paddle attachment and cream on medium speed for about 3 minutes, until very smooth with no visible chunks of butter.

Use a silicone spatula to scrape down the bowl, then add the flour mixture and olives all at once and mix on low speed until completely incorporated. Remove the dough from the bowl and shape into a triangular log approximately 1¾ inches in diameter. Wrap tightly in plastic wrap and refrigerate for at least 40 minutes You can mix and shape the dough up to 2 days in advance and store it in the refrigerator until you intend to bake the cookies. Alternatively, you may freeze the dough for up to 3 months, then let it thaw in the refrigerator overnight before proceeding with the recipe.

Preheat your oven to 350°F. Line two baking sheets with parchment paper.

Remove the dough from the refrigerator, unwrap it, and place on a cutting board. Using a sharp chef's knife, slice the cookies about ¼ inch thick. Carefully transfer them to the parchment-lined baking sheets.

Place the baking sheets in the oven and bake for 16 to 18 minutes, until the edges are just slightly golden.

Remove the baking sheets from the oven and transfer the cookies to wire racks to cool. Store the cookies in an airtight container for up to 1 week.

Another cocktail-inspired cookie, these shortbreads contain just enough rum in the icing and the dough to make you feel a tiny bit tipsy. I can guarantee they'll be the first ones to disappear from the holiday cookie plate. Oh, what fun! ❤

BUTTERED RUM SHORTBREAD

Makes 36 cookies

SHORTBREAD DOUGH

2¼ cups all-purpose flour

½ teaspoon ground cinnamon

½ teaspoon ground nutmeg

¼ teaspoon ground cloves

½ teaspoon kosher salt

1 cup (2 sticks) unsalted butter, at room temperature

¾ cup powdered sugar

2 tablespoons dark or spiced rum

½ teaspoon pure vanilla extract

RUM ICING

¾ cup powdered sugar, plus more as needed

2 teaspoons coconut oil, melted

2 teaspoons dark or spiced rum

2 tablespoons heavy cream, plus more as needed, at room temperature

¼ teaspoon kosher salt

⅛ teaspoon ground cloves

1½ teaspoons crushed, dried, edible rose petals

Mix the dough: In a medium bowl, whisk together the flour, cinnamon, nutmeg, cloves, and salt. Set aside.

Place the butter and powdered sugar in the bowl of a stand mixer fitted with the paddle attachment and cream on medium speed for about 3 minutes, until very smooth with no visible chunks of butter.

Use a silicone spatula to scrape down the bowl, then add the rum and vanilla and mix until just incorporated. Add the flour mixture all at once and mix on low speed until completely incorporated. Remove the dough from the bowl and shape into a cylindrical log approximately 1½ inches in diameter. Wrap tightly in plastic wrap and refrigerate for at least 40 minutes. You can mix and shape the dough up to 2 days in advance and store it in the refrigerator until 1 hour before you intend to roll out the dough. Alternatively, you may freeze the dough for up to 3 months, then let it thaw in the refrigerator overnight before proceeding with the recipe.

Preheat your oven to 350°F. Line two baking sheets with parchment paper.

Remove the dough from the refrigerator, unwrap it, and place on a cutting board. Using a sharp chef's knife, slice the cookies about ¼ inch thick. Carefully transfer them to the parchment-lined baking sheets.

Place the baking sheets in the oven and bake for 14 to 16 minutes, until the edges are just slightly golden.

Remove the baking sheets from the oven and transfer the cookies to wire racks to cool.

CONTINUED

Make the icing: While cookies are cooling, in a medium bowl whisk together the powdered sugar, coconut oil, rum, cream, salt, and cloves until very smooth. The texture should remind you of Elmer's glue. Yum! If the icing seems a little dry, whisk in a bit more heavy cream. If it seems a little too wet, whisk in powdered sugar, 1 tablespoon at a time. Stir in the rose petals.

Once the cookies have fully cooled, use a small offset spatula or knife to spread a very thin, even layer of icing across the tops of the cookies. It should be carefully smoothed, not gloppy. Return the cookies to the baking sheets to give the icing a chance to set up before serving. Store the iced cookies in an airtight container for up to 1 week.

We started making these flaky little cookies as a way to use up the ridiculous amount of pie dough scraps we acquire. As a baker at home, you might not end up with quite so many, but if you freeze them, they will accumulate over time. Every time you make a pie, flatten your scraps after rolling out and wrap them tightly in plastic. Store the packs in the freezer, transferring them to your refrigerator one full day before you intend to make these cookies. The other option? Mix up a batch of our All-Butter Pie Dough (page 25) and use it for this recipe.

For the buttercream and cream cheese fillings, feel free to use any items you have lying around the pantry after baking from this book. Jasmine tea flowers, rose flower water, ground nuts, finely minced herbs paired with citrus zest, and chocolate chips are all good choices. You could even sandwich these little cookies together with some peanut butter or whipped cream and they'd be delicious. Some flavors, such as rose flower water, pack a bigger punch than others, which is why I give a measurement range of ½ teaspoon to 2 teaspoons—you'll want to taste as you go to get the flavoring right. ♥

PIE SANDWICH COOKIES

Makes 32 sandwich cookies from one full batch of pie dough
(or more, depending on the amount of scraps)

COOKIES

All your packaged pie dough scraps or 1 batch All-Butter Pie Dough (page 25)

1 large egg, beaten

2 tablespoons Sugar-Sugar (see page 12)

BUTTERCREAM FILLING (OPTIONAL)

½ cup (1 stick) unsalted butter, at room temperature

2 cups powdered sugar

½ to 2 teaspoons flavoring ingredients (see recipe introduction)

¼ teaspoon kosher salt

CREAM CHEESE FILLING (OPTIONAL)

¼ cup cream cheese, at room temperature

½ cup (1 stick) unsalted butter, at room temperature

2 to 2½ cups powdered sugar

Roll out and bake the cookies: Line one or more baking sheets with parchment paper. To roll out the dough, lightly flour your work surface and place the unwrapped pie dough scraps in the center. Following the directions in The Crust (see page 44), roll out the dough as for a pie crust. Using a 2-inch round cutter, cut the dough into rounds and lay them on the baking sheets. Wrap the sheets in plastic wrap and refrigerate until cold and firm.

Preheat your oven to 450°F.

Brush the dough rounds with the egg and sprinkle lightly with the Sugar-Sugar. Transfer the baking sheets to the oven and bake for 10 to 15 minutes, until the cookies rise and turn deep golden brown. Remove from the oven and set on wire racks to cool while you prepare the filling of your choice.

Make the buttercream or cream cheese filling: For the buttercream, combine the butter, powdered sugar, flavoring, and salt in the bowl of a stand mixer fitted with the paddle attachment and cream until very smooth. For the cream cheese filling, combine the cream cheese and butter with the remaining ingredients and continue as for the buttercream.

CONTINUED

½ to 2 teaspoons flavoring ingredients (see recipe introduction)

¼ teaspoon kosher salt

GANACHE FILLING (OPTIONAL)

½ cup heavy cream

4 ounces bittersweet, milk, or white chocolate, coarsely chopped

Make the ganache filling: In a heatproof bowl set over a saucepan of simmering water, combine the cream and chocolate pieces. Stir with a silicone spatula until completely melted and smooth.

Place half of the baked pie crust rounds bottom side up on the baking sheet. For all fillings, use a knife to spread a teaspoon or two of filling on top of each round, or scrape the filling into a pastry bag and pipe it onto the rounds. Top each with another cookie and gently press together to make sweet sandwich love.

Pie sandwich cookies are best eaten the day they're assembled. Store any leftovers in the fridge in an airtight container or tightly wrapped in plastic.

When January came after Sister Pie's first holiday season, I had some free time to experiment in the kitchen. I knew two things for sure: any good bakery needs a signature chocolate chip cookie recipe, and I was feeling obsessive about buckwheat. I played around with proportions of all-purpose flour to buckwheat flour in an attempt to create that perfect balance of texture and flavor. My mother, a captive audience while I scurried around her kitchen, strongly suggested that I make the cookie gluten-free, as she was trying that on for size in her own diet. Uncharacteristically, I followed her request. (I'm a free spirit, but I'm also an alternative flour–loving spirit.)

Holy cow! The cookie went from pretty darn good to uniquely and addictively delicious. These might be both my biggest source of recipe-development pride and my favorite treat to sneak from the bakery counter. (Consider storing a few of the baked cookies in the freezer. We've survived many sleepless nights in the kitchen on these frozen cookies alone.) I'm thrilled to share this recipe with you here on these pages. Thanks, Mom. ❤

BUCKWHEAT CHOCOLATE CHIP COOKIES

Makes 18 cookies

2¾ cups buckwheat flour

¼ cup shredded, unsweetened coconut

1½ teaspoons baking powder

1 teaspoon baking soda

1½ teaspoons kosher salt

¼ teaspoon ground cinnamon

½ cup (1 stick) unsalted butter, at room temperature

½ cup coconut oil, at room temperature

¾ cup packed light brown sugar

¾ cup granulated sugar

2 large eggs, at room temperature

2 teaspoons pure vanilla extract

8 ounces bittersweet chocolate chips (we use a 61% Callebaut)

Flaky sea salt, for sprinkling tops

In a medium bowl, gently whisk together the buckwheat flour, coconut, baking powder, baking soda, kosher salt, and cinnamon. Set aside.

Place the butter, coconut oil, and brown and granulated sugars in the bowl of a stand mixer fitted with the paddle attachment and cream on medium speed until homogeneous and paste-like, about 4 minutes. You will see the mixture change from grainy and wet to fluffy and voluminous.

Next, add the eggs and vanilla and mix until fully combined, about 2 minutes. Scrape the bowl thoroughly using a silicone spatula, being sure to reach underneath the paddle.

Add the flour mixture slowly and mix on low speed until the flour is almost completely incorporated—you should still be able to see some streaks of flour. Add the chocolate chips and mix until just combined. If you notice any flour at the bottom of the bowl, use your spatula to finish the mixing process.

CONTINUED

COOKIE PIE

Vintage Sister Pie fans will tell you that the Buckwheat Chocolate Chip Cookie Pie is a special kind of animal. To make it, fill a blind-baked shell with the raw cookie dough and bake in a preheated 350°F oven until the dough puffs up and cracks all across the top. Set on a wire rack to cool, then cut into wedges.

Scrape the cookie dough from the bowl onto a big sheet of plastic wrap. Wrap the dough tightly and transfer to your refrigerator, where it should rest for at least 24 hours and up to 3 days. Alternatively, you may freeze the dough for up to 3 months, then let it thaw on the kitchen counter overnight before proceeding with the recipe.

Preheat your oven to 350°F. Line two baking sheets with parchment paper.

Take the dough out of the refrigerator 2 to 3 hours before you plan to bake the cookies. Once it's pretty darn soft, use a ¼-cup measure or #20 (yellow) scoop to portion the dough into 2-inch balls. Place on the parchment-lined baking sheets. Slightly flatten each cookie with your palm and top with a few flakes of sea salt.

Transfer the baking sheets to the oven and bake for 16 to 18 minutes, until the edges are just slightly golden.

Remove the baking sheets from the oven and transfer the cookies to wire racks to cool. Store in an airtight container for up to 5 days.

FOR ROOM-TEMPERATURE COCONUT OIL

The melting point of coconut oil is very low—a jar left out in a hot kitchen will turn to liquid. Kept in the fridge, it becomes a solid mass that is difficult to scrape out with a spoon. This recipe calls for the coconut oil to be at room temperature, but that is not as easily achieved as it would be with butter. If your coconut oil is in a liquid state, simply portion what you need for the recipe into a bowl and stick it in the fridge. Check it every 10 minutes, stirring to see if it is uniformly malleable enough to scoop—it should be between a fully solid and a fully liquid state.

After the bakery opened, the Buckwheat Chocolate Chip was our only scooped cookie. I feel envious of my former self when I think about the blank slate of cookie opportunity that lay in front of me back then. It was my civic duty to come up with new cookie recipes, and my dad's peanut butter cookie cravings had some influence on the direction I took.

Knowing I'd never make just any ol' peanut butter cookie, my dad teased me with a few ideas. Mission accepted. This cookie's soft, salty-sweet, chewy center is spiked with smoked paprika and topped with a big pinch of flaky sea salt, raw sugar, and even more smoked paprika. The Peanut Butter Paprika Cookie represents our style at its best: familiar yet new, comforting with a side of adventure. ♥

PEANUT BUTTER PAPRIKA COOKIES

Makes 20 cookies

2 cups all-purpose flour

⅓ cup whole wheat flour

1½ teaspoons baking powder

1 teaspoon baking soda

1½ teaspoons kosher salt

3 teaspoons smoked paprika

1 cup (2 sticks) unsalted butter, at room temperature

1¼ cups creamy peanut butter

¾ cup packed light brown sugar

¾ cup granulated sugar

2 large eggs, at room temperature

2 teaspoons pure vanilla extract

2½ teaspoons smoked paprika

1½ teaspoons flaky sea salt

2 tablespoons Sugar-Sugar (see page 12)

Mix the dough: In a medium bowl, gently whisk together the all-purpose and whole wheat flours, baking powder, baking soda, kosher salt, and ½ teaspoon of the smoked paprika. Set aside.

Place the butter, peanut butter, and brown and granulated sugars in the bowl of a stand mixer fitted with the paddle attachment and cream on medium speed until homogeneous and paste-like, about 4 minutes. You will see the mixture change from grainy and wet to fluffy and voluminous.

Next add the eggs and vanilla and mix until fully combined, about 2 minutes. Scrape the bowl thoroughly using a silicone spatula, being sure to reach underneath the paddle.

Add the flour mixture slowly and mix on low speed until the flour is completely incorporated. If you notice any flour at the bottom of the bowl, use your spatula to finish the mixing process.

Scrape the cookie dough from the bowl onto a big sheet of plastic wrap. Wrap the dough tightly and transfer to your refrigerator, where it should rest for at least 24 hours and up to 3 days. Alternatively, you may freeze the dough for up to 3 months, then let it thaw on the kitchen counter overnight before proceeding with the recipe.

Preheat your oven to 350°F. Line two baking sheets with parchment paper.

CONTINUED

Take the dough out of the refrigerator 2 to 3 hours before you plan to bake the cookies. Once it's pretty darn soft, use a ¼-cup measure or #20 (yellow) scoop to portion the dough into 2-inch balls. Place on the baking sheets. Slightly flatten each cookie with your palm, then use a fork to do that classic peanut butter cookie # design.

In a small bowl, combine the remaining 2½ teaspoons paprika, the sea salt, and Sugar-Sugar. Top each cookie with about ½ teaspoon of the paprika mixture. Transfer the baking sheets to the oven and bake for 16 to 18 minutes, until the edges are beginning to turn golden brown and the tops don't look wet at all.

Remove the baking sheets from the oven and transfer the cookies to wire racks to cool. Store in an airtight container for up to 5 days.

I started making snickerdoodles when I was working part-time as a nanny for two super-cool kids, Maeve and Carson. They were witnesses to my burgeoning culinary pursuits and eager taste-testers, too! Carson's favorite was the classic snickerdoodle, with its cinnamon-sugar dip and tangy chew. When it came time to create our own version, we wanted it to be not-so-classic. The result is refreshing and unexpected. ♥

FENNEL SEED SNICKERDOODLES

Makes 36 cookies

2½ cups all-purpose flour

2 teaspoons cream of tartar

1 teaspoon baking soda

¼ teaspoon kosher salt

¼ cup fennel seeds, toasted until fragrant (see page 35)

½ cup sesame seeds, toasted until fragrant (see page 35)

1 cup (2 sticks) unsalted butter, at room temperature

¾ cup packed light brown sugar

1 cup granulated sugar

2 large eggs, at room temperature

½ teaspoon ground cinnamon

½ cup Sugar-Sugar (see page 12)

¼ teaspoon flaky sea salt

In a medium bowl, gently whisk together the flour, cream of tartar, baking soda, kosher salt, and fennel and sesame seeds.

Place the butter and light brown and granulated sugars in the bowl of a stand mixer fitted with the paddle attachment and cream on medium speed until homogeneous and paste-like, about 4 minutes. You will see the mixture change from grainy and wet to fluffy and voluminous.

Next, add the eggs and mix until fully combined, about 2 minutes. Scrape the bowl thoroughly using a silicone spatula or bowl scraper, being sure to reach underneath the paddle.

Add the flour mixture slowly and mix on low speed until the flour is completely incorporated.

Scrape the cookie dough from the bowl onto a big sheet of plastic wrap. Wrap the dough tightly and transfer to your refrigerator, where it should rest for at least 24 hours and up to 3 days. Alternatively, you may freeze the dough for up to 3 months, then let it thaw in the refrigerator overnight before proceeding with the recipe.

Preheat your oven to 350°F. Line two baking sheets with parchment paper.

In a small bowl, mix together the cinnamon, Sugar-Sugar, and sea salt.

Take the dough out of the refrigerator 2 to 3 hours before baking. Once it's pretty darn soft, use a 1½-tablespoon measure or a #40 (purple) scoop to portion the dough into 1-inch balls, and roll them in the cinnamon-sugar mixture. Place on the baking sheets. Transfer the baking sheets to the oven and bake for 12 to 14 minutes, until the tops of the cookies begin to crack.

Remove the baking sheets from the oven and transfer the cookies to wire racks to cool. Store in an airtight container for up to 5 days.

When I was writing this book in a coffee shop one day, I was tempted to drive over to Sister Pie, stuff a bag with oaties, and drive back to the coffee shop. That's what this cookie will do to you. ♥

GOLDEN OATIE COOKIES

Makes 24 cookies

1¼ cups all-purpose flour

¾ cup whole wheat flour

2½ cups rolled oats

1½ teaspoons baking powder

1 teaspoon baking soda

1½ teaspoons kosher salt

½ teaspoon cinnamon

1 teaspoon ground ginger

1 cup (2 sticks) unsalted butter, at room temperature

¾ cup packed light brown sugar

¾ cup granulated sugar

2 large eggs, at room temperature

2 teaspoons pure vanilla extract

2 cups golden raisins

Flaky sea salt, for sprinkling tops

In a medium bowl, gently whisk together the all-purpose and whole wheat flours, oats, baking powder, baking soda, kosher salt, cinnamon, and ginger. Set aside.

Place the butter and brown and granulated sugars in the bowl of a stand mixer fitted with the paddle attachment and cream on medium speed until homogeneous and paste-like, about 4 minutes. You will see the mixture change from grainy and wet to fluffy and voluminous.

Next, add the eggs and vanilla and mix until fully combined, about 2 minutes. Scrape the bowl thoroughly using a silicone spatula or bowl scraper (or your hand), being sure to reach underneath the paddle.

Add the flour mixture slowly and mix on low speed until the flour is almost completely incorporated. Add the raisins and mix until just combined. If you notice any flour at the bottom of the bowl, use your spatula to finish the mixing process.

Scrape the cookie dough from the bowl onto a big sheet of plastic wrap. Wrap the dough tightly and transfer to your refrigerator, where it should rest for at least 24 hours and up to 3 days. Alternatively, you may freeze the dough for up to 3 months, then let it thaw on the kitchen counter overnight before proceeding with the recipe.

Preheat your oven to 350°F. Line two baking sheets with parchment paper.

Take the dough out of the refrigerator 2 to 3 hours before you plan to bake the cookies. Once it's pretty darn soft, use a ¼-cup measure or #20 (yellow) scoop to portion the dough into 2-inch balls. Place on the baking sheets. Slightly flatten each cookie with your palm and top with a few flakes of sea salt. Transfer the baking sheets to the oven and bake for 16 to 18 minutes, until the edges are just slightly golden.

Remove the baking sheets from the oven and transfer the cookies to wire racks to cool. Store in an airtight container for up to 5 days.

One of my favorite parts about owning a bakery is getting to name things. The fridges, the freezers, the pies, the cookies, the list goes on. When I introduced this cookie during the pie shop's first fall season, my employees rolled their eyes at me while I giggled like a maniac at the thought of customers trying to spit out the full name and stay straight-faced. I picked the name to say, *Hey, you might think these cookies are chocolate-y, but you actually have no idea, because guess what? There are three forms of chocolate in here!*

A note on the triple-chocolate action: we make these cookies with Valrhona cocoa powder and Callebaut bittersweet and white chocolates. If you're thinking that white chocolate isn't technically chocolate, you're right, but I'd recommend you stop caring about that for the sake of this delicious cookie and its absolutely fantastic, borderline-insane name.

Unlike our other scooped cookies, these should be mixed, scooped, and baked the same day. A rest in the fridge makes them nearly impossible to scoop, unless you leave them out to soften for many hours in advance. ♥

DOUBLE-AND-BY-DOUBLE-I-MEAN-TRIPLE-CHOCOLATE COOKIES

Makes 18 cookies

6 ounces white chocolate, chopped

2⅓ cups bittersweet chocolate chips

2⅔ cups all-purpose flour

½ cup cocoa powder

1½ teaspoons baking powder

1 teaspoon baking soda

1½ teaspoons kosher salt

1 cup (2 sticks) unsalted butter, at room temperature

¾ cup granulated sugar

¾ cup packed light brown sugar

2 large eggs, at room temperature

2 teaspoons pure vanilla extract

1 cup large flake coconut

Flaky sea salt, for sprinkling tops

In a heatproof bowl set over a saucepan of simmering water, place 4 ounces of the chopped white chocolate and 1⅓ cups of the bittersweet chocolate chips. Whisk until melted. You'll want to do this step first so the chocolate has a chance to cool before being adding to the cookie dough.

In a medium bowl, gently whisk together the flour, cocoa powder, baking powder, baking soda, and kosher salt. Set aside.

Place the butter and granulated and brown sugars in the bowl of a stand mixer fitted with the paddle attachment and cream on medium speed until homogeneous and paste-like, about 4 minutes. You will see the mixture change from grainy and wet to fluffy and voluminous.

Next, add the eggs and vanilla and mix until fully combined, about 2 minutes. Scrape the bowl thoroughly using a silicone spatula or bowl scraper, being sure to reach underneath the paddle. Slowly pour in the cooled melted chocolate mixture and mix on low speed until combined.

CONTINUED

Add the flour mixture slowly and mix on low speed until the flour is almost completely incorporated. Add the remaining 1 cup chocolate chips, the remaining 2 ounces chopped white chocolate, and the coconut flakes and mix until just combined.

Preheat your oven to 350°F. Line two baking sheets with parchment paper.

Use a ¼-cup measure or #20 (yellow) scoop to portion the dough into 2-inch balls. Place on the baking sheets. Slightly flatten each cookie with your palm and top with a few flakes of the sea salt.

Transfer the baking sheets to the oven and bake for 16 to 18 minutes, until the cookies begin to crack on top.

Remove the baking sheets from the oven and transfer the cookies to wire racks to cool. Store in an airtight container for up to 5 days.

These sweet little snowballs are coconutty to their core, and are a favorite of both children and adults alike. Straightforward and simple, this recipe can be adjusted to make any kind of drop cookie imaginable. ♥

COCONUT DROPS

Makes 36 cookies

DOUGH
2½ cups all-purpose flour

½ teaspoon baking powder

¼ teaspoon kosher salt

1 cup (2 sticks) unsalted butter, at room temperature

½ cup powdered sugar

½ cup granulated sugar

¼ cup full-fat canned coconut milk

WHITE CHOCOLATE ICING
¾ cup chopped white chocolate

1 tablespoon coconut oil

¼ cup heavy cream

1 cup powdered sugar

1 cup shredded, unsweetened coconut

Make the dough: In a medium bowl, gently whisk together the flour, baking powder, and salt. Set aside.

Place the butter and powdered and granulated sugars in the bowl of a stand mixer fitted with the paddle attachment and cream on medium speed for about 3 minutes, until very smooth with no visible chunks of butter.

Add the coconut milk and mix until fully combined. Scrape the bowl thoroughly, add the flour mixture all at once, and mix on low speed until a dough forms.

Scrape the cookie dough from the bowl onto a big sheet of plastic wrap. Wrap the dough tightly and transfer to your refrigerator, where it should rest for at least 24 hours and up to 3 days. Alternatively, you may freeze the dough for up to 3 months, then let it thaw in the refrigerator overnight before proceeding with the recipe.

Preheat your oven to 350°F. Line two baking sheets with parchment paper.

Take the dough out of the refrigerator 2 to 3 hours before baking. Once the dough is pretty darn soft, use a 1½-tablespoon measure or a #40 (purple) scoop to portion the dough into 1-inch balls. Place on the baking sheets. Transfer the baking sheets to the oven and bake for 12 to 14 minutes, until the bottom edges of the cookies are beginning to turn golden brown.

Remove the baking sheets from the oven and transfer the cookies to wire racks to cool.

Make the icing: In a heatproof bowl set over a saucepan of simmering water, combine the white chocolate and coconut oil. Whisk until melted, stir in the cream, and remove from the heat to cool slightly. Add the powdered sugar to the white chocolate mixture and whisk until very smooth.

CONTINUED

Place the coconut in a small bowl and set it next to the icing.

Once the cookies have fully cooled, pick up one at a time, and dunk, top side down, into the bowl of white chocolate icing. You will almost completely cover the cookie dome. Hold the cookie over the bowl for a second or two to allow the excess icing to run off. Turn the cookie upright for a moment, and then immediately dip it into the coconut, fully coating the icing. Return the cookie to the baking sheet and repeat with the rest of the cookies.

Let the icing set up before serving. Store iced cookies in an airtight container for up to 1 week.

The improvisational need that arises from mistakes and/or unforeseen issues is one of my favorite parts about running a bakery, being a cook, and, well, living. These cookies were born of an inventory hiccup. One of our pastry cooks, Kara, was in the middle of mixing a batch of Golden Oatie Cookies (page 169) when she realized we didn't have nearly enough raisins to complete the recipe. Whoops! A grin stretched across my face and I immediately thought, *How exciting*. I ran across the street to the market, grabbed a bag of pretzels, and ran back inside the bakery to find chocolate chips and walnuts. We threw 'em all in the mix and the Robert Redford Cookie was born.

You might recognize that these cookies are very similar to the classic cowboy cookie, except with pretzels instead of coconut. Crunchy, salty, chewy, chocolatey.

Why the name? There's no real reason, other than that I thought it'd be fun to name the cookie after a movie star. More improvisation, I suppose. Anji and Kamaria enthusiastically fought to name them for good, strong, all-around stand-up guy and certified dreamboat Robert Redford. Cowboy cookie, indeed. ♥

ROBERT REDFORD COOKIES

Makes 18 cookies

1¼ cups all-purpose flour

½ cup whole wheat flour

2 cups rolled oats

1½ teaspoons baking powder

1 teaspoon baking soda

1½ teaspoons kosher salt

⅛ teaspoon ground cinnamon

⅛ teaspoon ground nutmeg

1 cup (2 sticks) unsalted butter, at room temperature

¾ cup packed light brown sugar

¾ cup granulated sugar

2 large eggs, at room temperature

2 teaspoons pure vanilla extract

1 cup broken pretzel rods (½-inch pieces)

In a medium bowl, gently whisk together the all-purpose and whole wheat flours, oats, baking powder, baking soda, kosher salt, cinnamon, and nutmeg. Set aside.

Place the butter and brown and granulated sugars in the bowl of a stand mixer fitted with the paddle attachment and cream on medium speed until homogeneous and paste-like, about 4 minutes. You will see the mixture change from grainy and wet to fluffy and voluminous.

Add the eggs and vanilla and mix on medium speed until fully combined, about 2 minutes. Scrape the bowl thoroughly using a silicone spatula or bowl scraper, being sure to reach underneath the paddle.

Add the flour mixture slowly and mix on low speed until the flour is almost completely incorporated. Add the pretzels, chopped chocolate, and walnuts and mix until just combined.

1 cup chopped milk chocolate (from your favorite bar)

½ cup coarsely chopped toasted walnuts (see page 35)

Flaky sea salt, for sprinkling tops

Scrape the cookie dough from the bowl onto a big sheet of plastic wrap. Wrap the dough tightly and transfer to your refrigerator, where it should rest for at least 24 hours and up to 3 days. Alternatively, you may freeze the dough for up to 3 months, then let it thaw in the refrigerator overnight before proceeding with the recipe.

Preheat your oven to 350°F. Line two baking sheets with parchment paper.

Take the dough out of the refrigerator 2 to 3 hours before baking. Once it's pretty darn soft, use a ¼-cup measure or a #20 (yellow) scoop to portion the dough into 2-inch balls. Place on the baking sheets. Slightly flatten each cookie with your palm and top with a few flakes of the sea salt. Transfer the baking sheets to the oven and bake for 16 to 18 minutes, until the edges are just slightly golden.

Remove the baking sheets from the oven and transfer the cookies to wire racks to cool. Store in an airtight container for up to 5 days.

The best brownies always have silly names, like killer or sinful or drop-dead delicious. One recipe tester, Hilary, said it better than I could (or would): "This brownie is firing on all cylinders. It looks like outer space, I love it so much. I love the buckwheat notes, I love the coconut bits and the chocolate chips, I love the fudgy texture. Then the whole time you're thinking, 'There's PUMPKIN in here!' Everything works. It is pretty intense, but that's a brownie! One more thing: I love these." They're gluten-free, they're vegan, and they're from another galaxy. ♥

FROM ANOTHER GALAXY (GLUTEN-FREE, VEGAN) BROWNIES

Makes 16 brownies

2½ cups buckwheat flour

1 cup cocoa powder

1 cup shredded, unsweetened coconut

1¼ teaspoons kosher salt

1 teaspoon baking powder

1 teaspoon ground cinnamon

1 (15-ounce) can pumpkin puree

½ cup canola oil or other neutral oil

2½ cups plus 1 tablespoon turbinado sugar

½ cup almond milk, plain and unsweetened (or other nondairy milk)

4 teaspoons pure vanilla extract

½ cup coconut oil

1½ cups nondairy chocolate chips (preferably bittersweet)

1 tablespoon flaky sea salt

Preheat your oven to 350°F. Line a 9 by 13-inch baking pan with parchment paper, leaving an overhang of 1 or 2 inches so you can easily lift the brownies out of the pan after cooling.

Let's make some brownies! In a large bowl, whisk together the buckwheat flour, cocoa powder, shredded coconut, kosher salt, baking powder, and cinnamon. In another large bowl, combine the pumpkin, canola oil, 2½ cups of the turbinado sugar, the almond milk, and vanilla. Whisk until smooth.

In a heatproof bowl set over a saucepan of simmering water, combine the coconut oil and 1 cup of the chocolate chips. Stir with a silicone spatula until the chips are completely melted. Set aside to cool slightly.

Whisk the chocolate mixture into the pumpkin mixture until combined. Next, begin to add the flour mixture in two parts, using the spatula to gently fold the dry ingredients into the wet mixture. Add the remaining ½ cup chocolate chips with the second addition of flour, continuing to fold until completely incorporated.

Use the silicone spatula to transfer the brownie batter to the baking pan. Evenly spread the batter across the pan using an offset spatula, making sure to smooth the surface from edge to edge. Sprinkle the sea salt and remaining 1 tablespoon turbinado sugar over the top.

Place the pan in the oven and bake for 40 to 45 minutes, until the edges have begun to rise and crack and the center feels set when touched.

Remove the pan from the oven and place on a wire rack to cool. Once the bottom of the pan is at room temperature, place the pan in the freezer for a 15-minute rest. Carefully lift the brownies out of the pan and onto a cutting board, using the parchment overhang for handles. You may need to use a knife to loosen the sides of the brownies before attempting to lift them. Use a sharp chef's knife to slice into 16 pieces.

I've never been a big blondie fan, although I have a special place in my heart for the time that Veronica Mars belted out "One Way or Another" at karaoke. I've always found them to be unbalanced, even with the addition of chocolate chips, nuts, or other enhancements. Here we have the anti-blondie: The tart rhubarb (a vegetable!) contrasts starkly with the super sweetness of regular blondie players like brown sugar and white chocolate. The almonds contribute to even more textural diversity, while the Sugar-Sugar topping creates an almost crunchy, caramelized top layer. ♥

RHUBARB BLONDIES

Makes 9 blondies

1 cup sliced rhubarb (½-inch slices)

2 teaspoons granulated sugar

½ cup plus 2 tablespoons (1¼ sticks) unsalted butter, melted and cooled

½ cup packed light brown sugar

½ cup packed dark brown sugar

2 large eggs, at room temperature

1½ teaspoons pure vanilla extract

1¼ cups all-purpose flour

1 teaspoon kosher salt

½ cup slivered almonds

½ cup chopped white chocolate

3 tablespoons Sugar-Sugar (see page 12)

Preheat your oven to 350°F. Line a greased 8-inch-square baking pan with parchment paper, leaving an overhang of 1 to 2 inches so you can easily lift the blondies out of the pan after cooling.

In a small bowl, mix the rhubarb with the granulated sugar and set aside.

In a large mixing bowl, combine the melted butter with the light and dark brown sugars and whisk until smooth. Use a silicone spatula to scrape down the sides and bottom of the mixing bowl. Add the eggs and vanilla and fold until smooth.

Add the flour and salt and stir until the flour is almost completely incorporated, then add the rhubarb-sugar mixture, almonds, and white chocolate and mix until just combined.

Use the spatula to scrape the blondie batter into the prepared pan, making sure to smooth the surface from edge to edge. Sprinkle the Sugar-Sugar over the top. Place the pan in the oven and bake for 25 to 30 minutes, until just set.

Remove the pan from the oven and place on a wire rack to cool. Once the bottom of the pan is at room temperature, carefully lift the blondies out of the pan and onto a cutting board, using the parchment overhang for handles. You may need to use a knife to loosen the sides of the blondies before attempting to lift.

Use a sharp chef's knife to slice the blondies into 9 bars. Store in an airtight container at room temperature for up to 4 days.

Seeing as I'm a person who doesn't particularly enjoy sitting down for long periods of time, I've long dreamt of opening a bed-and-breakfast in my post–Sister Pie years to keep up with my natural hustle and bustle. The act of making someone their first meal of the day brings me great joy, from frying up eggs at home to brushing the scones with cream before transferring them into the bakery ovens. Sometimes I think I got into this business just so I could serve breakfast. It's the creative baker's dream—the only meal where sweet and savory options are both totally acceptable. In this chapter, you'll find recipes for scones, muffins, paczki, and more. Many of them are seasonally inspired but completely adaptable, to be made with whatever you have on hand.

Every good bakery needs an addictively good granola. Ours is another testament to our buckwheat affinity, with its crunchy, nutty, sweet, and salty qualities. We sell it by the bag, and also serve it at the shop with tart, plain yogurt and a dollop of seasonal compote. It's equally good with any kind of milk (dairy or other) and half a banana. When I go that route, I like to let it sit for 10 minutes before chowing down so the grains soften and flavor the milk. ♥

SPRANOLA (AKA SISTER PIE GRANOLA)

Makes 9 cups granola

3 cups rolled oats

2 cups raw buckwheat groats

1¾ cups large flake coconut

1½ cups mixed nuts and/or seeds (we like to use pistachios, pepitas, and sunflower seeds)

¼ teaspoon ground allspice

¼ teaspoon ground cardamom

¼ teaspoon ground ginger

1 teaspoon ground cinnamon

1 tablespoon fennel seeds

1 tablespoon sesame seeds

1 tablespoon poppy seeds

1 teaspoon kosher salt

¾ cup Grade B maple syrup

1½ teaspoons pure vanilla extract

¼ cup packed light brown sugar

½ cup extra-virgin olive oil

⅓ cup coconut oil

Preheat your oven to 325°F. Line two baking sheets with parchment paper.

In a large bowl, combine the oats, buckwheat groats, coconut, mixed nuts or seeds, allspice, cardamom, ginger, cinnamon, fennel seeds, sesame seeds, poppy seeds, and salt and mix thoroughly. In a small saucepan over medium-low heat, combine the maple syrup, vanilla, brown sugar, olive oil, and coconut oil. Gently heat until the coconut oil is melted and the brown sugar is dissolved.

Pour the maple mixture over the oat mixture and combine thoroughly, using a silicone spatula.

Spread the mixture onto the parchment-lined baking sheets, dividing it evenly between the pans and pressing down on the granola with the spatula or the back of a measuring cup. Transfer the pans to the oven and bake for 55 minutes, or until the granola appears dry and set, with a slight sheen. Remove the baking sheets from the oven and set them on wire racks to cool. When the granola is completely cool, break it into pieces and transfer to an airtight container.

Store at room temperature for up to 2 weeks.

COCOA SPRANOLA

One recipe tester, Tim, informed me that we once offered a chocolate-y version of our granola. I still think he might be pulling a fast one, as I have no memory of it, but here it is. This version (pictured above) is how your favorite chocolate-y childhood cereal would taste if it grew up and joined a gym. To make it, add ¼ cup cocoa powder to the spice mix and increase the coconut oil by 3 tablespoons. Bake at 300°F (if you bake it at 325°F, as for the Spranola, you'll end up with burnt cocoa).

While clotted cream and piping-hot tea are natural accompaniments to the scone, sometimes it's more fun to eschew tradition. As you can see from the other flavors in this book, the scones at Sister Pie are anything but traditional. The Jasmine and Crème Fraîche Scone, however, harks back to that classic combination by including tea flowers and a thickened, fat-forward cream right in the scone dough. We use loose green jasmine tea. You could opt to do the same or find green jasmine tea bags. The larger the jasmine flowers the better, but any option will work in this scone.

These scones are best eaten warm with the rest of the crème fraiche. Invite your grandmother. ♥

JASMINE CRÈME FRAÎCHE SCONES

Makes 8 scones

½ cup heavy cream

¾ cup crème fraîche

1 large egg

2¾ cups all-purpose flour

1 tablespoon plus 2 teaspoons baking powder

2 tablespoons green jasmine tea leaves

¾ cup granulated sugar

2 teaspoons kosher salt

½ cup (1 stick) unsalted butter, straight from the fridge

¼ cup Sugar-Sugar (see page 12)

Preheat your oven to 425°F. Line a baking sheet with parchment paper.

In a small bowl, gently whisk together ¼ cup of the heavy cream, the crème fraîche, and egg.

In a large stainless steel bowl, combine the flour, baking powder, jasmine tea, sugar, and salt. Place the butter in the bowl and coat on all sides with flour. Use a bench scraper to cut the butter into ½-inch cubes. Work quickly to break up the cubes with your hands until they are all lightly coated in flour. Continue to use the bench scraper to cut the cubes into smaller pieces—the idea is that you are cutting each cube in half.

Switch to a pastry blender and begin to cut in the butter with one hand while turning the bowl with the other. It's important not to aim for the same spot at the bottom of the bowl with each movement, but to actually slice through butter every time to maximize efficiency. When the pastry blender clogs up, carefully clean it out with your fingers (watch out, it bites!) or a butter knife and use your hands to toss the ingredients a bit. Continue to blend and turn until most of the butter is incorporated but you still have quite a few larger chunks—think about the process of making pie dough (see page 25), and then stop before you get to the peas and Parmesan stage.

Pour the cream mixture into the dry ingredients. Use a silicone spatula to incorporate the wet ingredients into the flour mixture and mix until you no longer see pools of liquid. Using the tips of your fingers (and a whole lot of pressure), turn the dough over and press it back into itself a few times. With each effort, rotate the bowl and try to scoop up as much of the dough as possible, with the intention of quickly forming it into one cohesive mass. Remember to incorporate any dry, floury bits that have congregated at the bottom of the bowl. Once those are completely gone and the dough is formed, it's time to stop.

Turn the dough out onto a lightly floured surface, making sure to scrape every last bit from the bowl. Using extra flour as needed, pat the dough into an 8-inch circle, and use a bench scraper to cut the dough into 8 equal wedges. You can cut and form the scones in advance and freeze them for up to 3 months before baking. To do so, simply place the unbaked scones on the parchment-lined baking sheet and freeze for at least 1 hour. Once the scones are frozen solid, wrap them tightly in plastic wrap and return to the freezer.

Transfer the scones to the baking sheet, leaving at least 2 inches between them. Brush the tops with the remaining ¼ cup cream and sprinkle liberally with the Sugar-Sugar.

Place the baking sheet in the oven and bake for 18 to 25 minutes, until the scones are evenly golden brown and nearly doubled in size. If baking from frozen, decrease the oven temperature to 400°F and bake for 25 to 35 minutes. Test for doneness by gently pressing the top of a scone—it should spring back when done. Remove the baking sheet from the oven and transfer the scones to a wire rack to cool.

While I highly recommend eating the scones only on the day they're baked, you can store leftovers under a pie dome for up to 2 days.

DIY CRÈME FRAÎCHE

When we make these scones at the bakery, we combine 1 cup cream with 2 tablespoons buttermilk and let it sit, covered, at room temperature overnight. Then we store it in the fridge until it's thickened and we're ready to make the scones. It's an easy, from-scratch ingredient that makes a big difference in the flavor of these scones, especially if you have delicious cream from a local dairy and have planned far enough in advance. If not, you can find little tubs of crème fraîche not far from the European-style butter in many grocery stores.

We're usually scrambling to maintain our pie fruit supply throughout the summer, so it feels like a special treat whenever we have enough to add fruit to our scones. We reduce the liquid in this recipe to account for the moisture from the juicy berries. These scones are best eaten warm with a big dollop of freshly whipped cream—kinda like a blueberry shortcake! ♥

BLUEBERRY CORNMEAL SCONES

Makes 8 scones

¾ cup heavy cream, plus more as needed

1 large egg

1¾ cups all-purpose flour

1 cup fine yellow cornmeal

1 tablespoon plus 2 teaspoons baking powder

¾ cup granulated sugar

2 teaspoons kosher salt

½ cup (1 stick) unsalted butter, straight from the fridge

2 cups fresh blueberries (frozen works fine, too)

¼ cup Sugar-Sugar (see page 12)

Preheat your oven to 425°F. Line a baking sheet with parchment paper.

In a small bowl, gently whisk ½ cup of the cream and the egg.

In a large stainless steel bowl, combine the flour, cornmeal, baking powder, granulated sugar, and salt. Place the butter in the bowl and coat on all sides with flour. Use a bench scraper to cut the butter into ½-inch cubes. Work quickly to break up the cubes with your hands until they are all lightly coated in flour. Continue to use the bench scraper to cut the cubes into smaller pieces—the idea is that you are cutting each cube in half.

Switch to a pastry blender and begin to cut in the butter with one hand while turning the bowl with the other. It's important not to aim for the same spot at the bottom of the bowl with each movement, but to actually slice through butter every time. When the pastry blender clogs up, carefully clean it out with your fingers

(watch out, it bites!) or a butter knife and use your hands to toss the ingredients a bit. Continue to blend and turn until most of the butter is incorporated but you still have quite a few larger chunks— think about the process of making pie dough (see page 25), and then stop before you get to the peas and Parmesan stage.

Add the blueberries and use your hands or the bench scraper to evenly toss them throughout the butter-flour mixture. Pour the cream mixture into the dry ingredients. Use a silicone spatula to incorporate it into the flour mixture, and mix until you no longer see pools of liquid. Using the tips of your fingers (and a whole lot of pressure), turn the dough over and press it back into itself a few times. With each effort, rotate the bowl and try to scoop up as much of the dough as possible, with the intention of quickly forming it into one cohesive mass. Remember to incorporate any dry, floury bits that have congregated at the bottom of the bowl. Once the dough is fully formed, it's time to stop! Note: if your scone dough feels too dry, add more cream, 1 tablespoon at a time. This recipe is dependent on the moisture content of the blueberries, so we start with the liquid on the low end in anticipation of that.

CONTINUED

Turn the dough out onto a lightly floured surface, making sure to scrape every last bit from the bowl. Using extra flour as needed, pat the dough into an 8-inch circle, and use a bench scraper to cut the dough into 8 equal wedges. You can form the scones in advance and freeze them for up to 3 months before baking. Simply place the unbaked scones on the parchment-lined baking sheet and freeze for at least 1 hour. Once the scones are frozen solid, wrap them tightly in plastic wrap and return to the freezer.

Transfer the scones to the baking sheet, leaving at least 2 inches between them. Brush the tops with the remaining ¼ cup cream and sprinkle liberally with the Sugar-Sugar.

Place the baking sheet in the oven and bake for 18 to 25 minutes, until the scones are evenly golden brown and nearly doubled in size. If baking from frozen, decrease the oven temperature to 400°F and bake for 25 to 35 minutes. You can test for doneness by gently pressing the top of a scone—it should spring back when done. Remove the baking sheet from the oven and transfer the scones to a wire rack to cool.

While I highly recommend eating the scones only on the day they're baked, you can store leftovers under a pie dome for up to 2 days.

The best kind of bread has a spongy, seed-speckled crumb with a crunchy, almost burnt crust. Spread with barely softened butter, it's a snack parade into your mouth. Here's that experience in scone form. Get 'em while they're hot!

The sour cream in these scones provides the richness needed for a tender crumb in a scone made with a whole-grain flour. ♥

SUNFLOWER SPELT SCONES

Makes 8 scones

¾ cup sour cream

½ cup heavy cream

1 large egg

1¾ cups all-purpose flour

1 cup spelt flour

1 cup salted sunflower seeds, toasted (see page 35)

1 tablespoon plus 2 teaspoons baking powder

2 teaspoons kosher salt

2 tablespoons granulated sugar

½ cup (1 stick) unsalted butter, straight from the fridge

Flaky sea salt, for sprinkling tops

Preheat your oven to 425°F. Line a baking sheet with parchment paper.

In a small bowl, gently whisk together the sour cream, ¼ cup of the heavy cream, and the egg.

In a large bowl, combine the all-purpose flour, spelt flour, ½ cup of the sunflower seeds, the baking powder, kosher salt, and sugar. Place the butter in the bowl and coat on all sides with flour. Use a bench scraper to cut the butter into ½-inch cubes. Work quickly to break up the cubes with your hands until they are all lightly coated in flour. Continue to use the bench scraper to cut the cubes into smaller pieces—the idea is that you are cutting each cube in half.

Switch to a pastry blender and begin to cut in the butter with one hand while turning the bowl with the other. It's important not to aim for the same spot at the bottom of the bowl with each movement, but to actually slice through butter every time to maximize efficiency. When the pastry blender clogs up, carefully clean it out with your fingers (watch out, it bites!) or a butter knife and use your hands to toss the ingredients a bit. Continue to blend and turn until most of the butter is incorporated but you still have quite a few larger chunks—think about the process of making pie dough (see page 25), and then stop before you get to the peas and Parmesan stage.

Pour the cream mixture into the dry ingredients. Use a silicone spatula to incorporate it into the flour mixture, and mix until you no longer see pools of liquid. Using the tips of your fingers (and a whole lot of pressure), turn the dough over and press it back into itself a few times. With each effort, rotate the bowl and try to scoop up as much of the dough as possible, with the

CONTINUED

intention of quickly forming it into one cohesive mass. Remember to incorporate any dry, floury bits that have congregated at the bottom of the bowl. Once the dough is fully formed, it's time to stop!

Turn the dough out onto a lightly floured surface, making sure to scrape every last bit from the bowl. Pat the dough into an 8-inch circle, and use the bench scraper to divide the dough into 8 equal wedges. You can form the scones in advance and freeze them for up to 3 months before baking. Simply place the unbaked scones on a parchment-lined baking sheet and freeze for at least 1 hour. Once the scones are frozen solid, wrap them tightly in plastic wrap and return to the freezer.

Transfer the scones to the baking sheet, leaving at least 2 inches between them. Brush the tops of the scones with the remaining ¼ cup heavy cream and sprinkle with the remaining ½ cup sunflower seeds and a few flakes of sea salt.

Place the baking sheet in the oven and bake for 18 to 25 minutes, until the scones are evenly golden brown and nearly doubled in size. If baking from frozen, decrease the oven temperature to 400°F and bake for 25 to 35 minutes. You can test for doneness by gently pressing the top of a scone—it should spring back when done. Remove the baking sheet from the oven and transfer the scones to a wire rack to cool.

These scones are best eaten warm, broken open and slathered with butter. While I highly recommend eating the scones on the day they're baked, you can store leftovers under a pie dome for up to 2 days.

I like breakfast pastries most when they're stuffed with stuff. While I don't underestimate the allure of a classic and straightforward scone, I do not tire of the endless ways we can incorporate seasonal fruits and vegetables, cheese, chocolates, and nuts into every baked good on the menu. The other pastry cooks at Sister Pie tend to give me funny looks when I show them how many quarts of chopped leeks or whole strawberries I want them to fit into a batch of our light, buttery scones. This scone is no exception, and is an ode to my favorite savory toast topping: a thick layer of cream cheese (an ingredient beloved by this Midwestern baker), thinly sliced radishes, and lots of minced fresh dill. ♥

CREAM CHEESE, RADISH, AND DILL SCONES

Makes 8 scones

1¼ cups heavy cream

1 large egg

2 cups all-purpose flour

¾ cup whole wheat flour

1 tablespoon plus 2 teaspoons baking powder

2 teaspoons kosher salt

2 tablespoons granulated sugar

½ cup (1 stick) unsalted butter, straight from the fridge

1 cup julienned radishes

4 ounces cream cheese, cold, cut into ½-inch pieces

½ cup minced fresh dill

Flaky sea salt, for sprinkling tops

Preheat your oven to 425°F. Line a baking sheet with parchment paper.

In a small bowl, gently whisk together 1 cup of the cream and the egg.

In a large stainless steel bowl, combine the all-purpose and whole wheat flours, baking powder, kosher salt, and sugar. Place the butter in the bowl and coat on all sides with flour. Use a bench scraper to cut the butter into ½-inch cubes. Work quickly to break up the cubes with your hands until they are all lightly coated in flour. Continue to use the bench scraper to cut the cubes into smaller pieces—the idea is that you are cutting each cube in half.

Switch to a pastry blender and begin to cut in the butter with one hand while turning the bowl with the other. It's important not to aim for the same spot at the bottom of the bowl with each movement, but to actually slice through butter every time for maximum efficiency. When the pastry blender clogs up, carefully clean it out with your fingers (watch out, it bites!) or a butter knife and use your hands to toss the ingredients a bit. Continue to blend and turn until most of the butter is incorporated but you still have quite a few larger chunks—think about the process of making pie dough (see page 25), and then stop before you get to the peas and Parmesan stage.

CONTINUED

Add the radishes, cream cheese, and dill and use your hands or the bench scraper to toss them evenly throughout the butter-flour mixture. Pour the cream mixture into the dry ingredients. Use a silicone spatula to incorporate it into the flour mixture, and mix until you no longer see pools of liquid. Using the tips of your fingers (and a whole lot of pressure), turn the dough over and press it back into itself a few times. With each effort, rotate the bowl and try to scoop up as much of the dough as possible, with the intention of quickly forming it into one cohesive mass. Remember to incorporate any dry, floury bits that have congregated at the bottom of the bowl. Once the dough is fully formed, it's time to stop!

Turn the dough out onto a lightly floured surface, making sure to scrape every last bit from the bowl. Pat the dough into an 8-inch circle, and use the bench scraper to divide the dough into 8 equal wedges. You can form the scones in advance and freeze them for up to 3 months before baking. Simply place the unbaked scones on the parchment-lined baking sheet and freeze for at least 1 hour. Once the scones are frozen solid, wrap them tightly in plastic wrap and return to the freezer.

Transfer the scones to the parchment-lined baking sheet, leaving at least 2 inches between them. Brush the tops of the scones with the remaining ¼ cup cream and sprinkle a few flakes of sea salt on each.

Place the baking sheet in the oven and bake for 18 to 25 minutes, until the scones are evenly golden brown and nearly doubled in size. If baking from frozen, decrease the oven temperature to 400°F and bake for 25 to 35 minutes. You can test for doneness by gently pressing the top of a scone—it should spring back when done. Remove the baking sheet from the oven and transfer the scones to a wire rack to cool.

These scones are best eaten warm, split open and slathered with more cream cheese. While I highly recommend eating the scones on the day they're baked, you can store leftovers under a pie dome for up to 2 days.

The Midwest is known for a lot of things, but super-sweet, juicy, and firm corn on the cob is one of its finest offerings. Best eaten fresh from the pot with an inappropriate amount of butter and salt, it was one of the first things I learned to really chow down on. Here's a distinctly different way to eat it. ♥

BUTTERED CORN SCONES

Makes 8 scones

2 ears corn, shucked and cleaned

¾ cup (1½ sticks) unsalted butter, straight from the fridge

1¼ cups heavy cream, cold

1 large egg

2 cups all-purpose flour

¾ cup fine cornmeal

1 tablespoon plus 2 teaspoons baking powder

2 teaspoons kosher salt

2 tablespoons granulated sugar

Flaky sea salt, for sprinkling tops

Stand one ear of corn in a large bowl with the skinnier end up. Use a very sharp knife to slice down along the cob, removing the corn as you go. Once the corn has been released into the bowl, run your knife upward in the opposite direction to catch the milky residue, and place that in the bowl with the corn. Repeat until all kernels are removed from both ears. This should yield 1½ to 1¾ cups of corn kernels. Whatever you end up with, use all of it.

Melt 2 tablespoons of the butter in a skillet over medium heat, then add the corn and sauté for 5 to 6 minutes, until the corn is bright yellow. Remove from the heat and scrape the corn into a single layer onto a baking sheet or plate. Set aside to cool while you begin the dough.

In a small bowl, gently whisk 1 cup of the cream and the egg.

Preheat your oven to 425°F. Line a baking sheet with parchment paper.

In a large stainless steel bowl, combine the flour, cornmeal, baking powder, kosher salt, and sugar. Place the remaining ½ cup plus 2 tablespoons cold butter in the bowl and coat on all sides with the flour mixture. Use a bench scraper to cut the butter into ½-inch cubes. Work quickly to break up the cubes with your hands until they are all lightly coated in flour. Continue to use the bench scraper to cut each cube in half.

Switch to a pastry blender and begin to cut in the butter with one hand while turning the bowl with the other. It's important not to aim for the same spot at the bottom of the bowl with each movement, but to actually slice through butter every time. When the pastry blender clogs up, carefully clean it out with your fingers (watch out, it bites!) or a butter knife and use your hands to toss the ingredients a bit. Continue to blend and turn until most of the butter

CONTINUED

is incorporated but you still have quite a few larger chunks—think about the process of making pie dough (see page 25), and then stop before you get to the peas and Parmesan stage.

Add the cooked, cooled corn and use your hands or the bench scraper to toss it evenly throughout the butter-flour mixture. Pour the cream mixture into the dry ingredients. Use a silicone spatula (or the bench scraper) to incorporate it into the flour mixture, and mix until you no longer see pools of liquid. Using the tips of your fingers (and a whole lot of pressure), turn the dough over and press it back into itself a few times. With each effort, rotate the bowl and try to scoop up as much of the dough as possible, with the intention of quickly forming it into one cohesive mass. Remember to incorporate any dry, floury bits that have congregated at the bottom of the bowl. Once the dough is fully formed, it's time to stop!

Turn the dough out onto a lightly floured surface, making sure to scrape every last bit from the bowl. Pat the dough into an 8-inch circle, and use the bench scraper to divide the dough into 8 equal wedges. You can form the scones in advance and freeze them for up to 3 months before baking. Simply place the unbaked scones on the parchment-lined baking sheet and freeze for at least 1 hour. Once the scones are frozen solid, wrap them tightly in plastic wrap and return to the freezer.

Transfer the scones to the parchment-lined baking sheet, leaving at least 2 inches between them. Brush the tops with the remaining ¼ cup cream and sprinkle each with a flake or two of sea salt.

Place the baking sheet in the oven and bake for 18 to 25 minutes, until the scones are evenly golden brown and nearly doubled in size. If baking from frozen, decrease the oven temperature to 400°F and bake for 25 to 35 minutes. You can test for doneness by gently pressing the top of a scone—it should spring back when done. Remove the baking sheet from the oven and transfer the scones to a wire rack to cool.

These scones are best while eaten warm, split open and slathered with butter. While I highly recommend eating the scones on the day they're baked, you can store leftovers under a pie dome for up to 2 days.

One our first front-of-house employees, Jane, left quite a legacy at Sister Pie. She's the type of person who makes visiting a pie shop just as good as the pie itself. Jane treated everyone with extra-special care and respect, from the regular customers to the bright-eyed newcomers, to the numerous plants strewn about the counter and hanging from the windows. During her interview, I learned that her main gig was as a costume designer and that she loved the combination of blackberry and peach. To welcome her back to work after a summer working in Italy, we made blackberry-peach muffins. The combination works even better in the slightly altered coffee cake version of our spiced, not-too-sweet muffin batter. Why? Fruit in every bite!

This wet batter bakes up best after an overnight rest in the fridge. The oats will absorb the liquids and the batter will thicken. If you don't have time to let the batter rest overnight, simply place it in the fridge to rest for at least 20 minutes. ♥

BLACKBERRY PEACH COFFEE CAKE, FOR JANE

Makes 12 servings

BATTER

1½ cups buttermilk

½ cup yogurt (we prefer to use full-fat plain Greek yogurt)

2 large eggs

½ cup canola oil

⅓ cup turbinado sugar

1½ teaspoons pure vanilla extract

1½ cups rolled oats

¾ cup whole wheat flour

¾ cup spelt flour

2¼ teaspoons baking powder

2¼ teaspoons baking soda

½ teaspoon kosher salt

½ teaspoon ground allspice

½ teaspoon ground cardamom

½ teaspoon ground ginger

Mix the batter: In a medium bowl, whisk the buttermilk, yogurt, eggs, canola oil, turbinado sugar, and vanilla until the ingredients are homogeneous and smooth. In a large mixing bowl, whisk together the oats, whole wheat and spelt flours, baking powder, baking soda, salt, allspice, cardamom, and ginger, then add the wet ingredients. Use a silicone spatula to gently fold in the wet ingredients until no dry spots remain. Cover the bowl with plastic wrap or a lid and place in the refrigerator overnight or for at least 20 minutes.

Make the streusel: Combine the flour, brown sugar, cinnamon, and salt in a large stainless steel bowl. Place the butter in the bowl and coat on all sides with the flour mixture. Use a bench scraper to cut the butter into ½-inch cubes directly into the flour mixture in the bowl. Work to break up the cubes with your hands until they are lightly coated with the flour mixture. Continue to use the bench scraper to cut the cubes into smaller pieces—the idea is that you are cutting each cube in half.

CONTINUED

STREUSEL

1½ cups all-purpose flour

¾ cup packed light brown sugar

1½ teaspoons ground cinnamon

½ teaspoon kosher salt

¾ cup (1½ sticks) unsalted butter, straight from the fridge

1½ cups sliced peaches (see page 76)

1 cup blackberries

6 ounces cream cheese, at room temperature, divided into 12 equal pieces

2 tablespoons Sugar-Sugar (see page 12)

Switch to a pastry blender and begin to cut in the butter with one hand while turning the bowl with the other. It's important not to aim for the same spot at the bottom of the bowl with each movement, but to actually slice through butter every time to maximize efficiency. Once most of the butter is incorporated, use your fingers to fully break down the butter until the streusel resembles wet sand. The streusel can be prepared up to 2 days in advance and stored in the refrigerator before assembling and baking.

Preheat your oven to 400°F. Line a 9 by 13-inch baking pan with parchment paper, leaving an overhang of 1 to 2 inches so you can easily lift the coffee cake out of the pan after cooling.

Use a silicone spatula to transfer the batter to the baking pan. Use a knife or offset spatula to evenly spread the batter across the pan, making sure to smooth it from edge to edge. Evenly cover the batter with the peaches and blackberries, then distribute the 12 pieces of cream cheese over the batter, placing 4 pieces across the long sides of the pan and 3 along the ends of the pan, and so forth. Sprinkle with the Sugar-Sugar, then use the offset spatula to gently press the cream cheese down into the batter. Cover with the streusel. It's okay if some of the fruit is still visible. In fact, it's better than okay.

Place the baking pan in the oven and bake for 35 to 40 minutes, until a knife inserted into the middle of the coffee cake comes out clean. Remove the pan from the oven and set it on a wire rack to cool. Once the bottom of the pan is at room temperature, carefully lift the coffee cake out of the pan and onto a cutting board, using the parchment overhang for handles.

Use a sharp chef's knife to cut the coffee cake into 16 pieces. Store leftover coffee cake in an airtight container in the refrigerator for up to 2 days.

This is a historic muffin, as far we're concerned. It's the first one we ever served when the bakery doors swung open back in 2015. It turns the basic-in-a-bad-way combination of pumpkin and cream cheese into a basic-in-a-good-way (read: accessible) sweet potato and cream cheese delight. We leave the sweet potatoes unpeeled and roast them tenderly in big chunks with a tiny bit of light brown sugar and olive oil. Once they're combined with cream cheese, our wholesome muffin batter, and a sandy, magical streusel, it's the breakfast of textural champions. I usually wait 5 minutes after they're out of the oven to bust one open, watch the steam escape, and eat it slowly, piece by piece.

You'll notice that this is a very wet batter. It bakes up best after an overnight rest in the fridge—that's what we do to get the best domed tops. The oats will absorb the liquids and the batter will thicken enough for care-free muffin assembly the next day. If you don't have time to let the batter rest overnight, simply place it in the fridge to rest for at least 20 minutes. ♥

SWEET POTATO STREUSEL MUFFINS

Makes 12 muffins

SWEET POTATOES

12 ounces sweet potatoes (skin on), scrubbed and chopped into ½-inch cubes

2 teaspoons olive oil

2 teaspoons light brown sugar

¼ teaspoon kosher salt

BATTER

1 cup buttermilk

⅓ cup yogurt (we prefer to use full-fat, plain Greek yogurt)

1 large egg

⅓ cup canola oil

¼ cup turbinado sugar

1 teaspoon pure vanilla extract

1 cup rolled oats

½ cup whole wheat flour

½ cup spelt flour

1½ teaspoons baking powder

1½ teaspoons baking soda

First, roast the sweet potatoes: Preheat your oven to 400°F. Place the sweet potato cubes on a baking sheet and toss evenly with the olive oil, brown sugar, and salt. Place in the oven and roast for 30 to 40 minutes, or until the sweet potatoes are fork-tender. Transfer the baking sheet to a wire rack to cool. You can prepare the sweet potatoes up to 2 days in advance and store in an airtight container in the refrigerator.

Mix the batter: In a medium bowl, whisk the buttermilk, yogurt, egg, canola oil, turbinado sugar, and vanilla until well mixed and smooth. In a large mixing bowl, combine the oats, whole wheat and spelt flours, baking powder, baking soda, salt, allspice, cinnamon, and ginger. Add the buttermilk mixture to the dry ingredients, using a silicone spatula to gently fold them together until no dry spots remain. Cover the bowl with plastic wrap or a lid and place in the refrigerator overnight or for at least 20 minutes.

While the muffin batter hydrates, make the streusel: Combine the flour, brown sugar, cinnamon, and salt in a large stainless steel bowl. Place the butter in the bowl and coat on all sides with the flour mixture. Use a bench scraper to cut the butter into ½-inch cubes directly into the flour mixture in the bowl. Work to break up the cubes with your hands until they are lightly coated with the flour mixture. Continue to use the bench scraper to cut the cubes into smaller pieces—the idea is that you are cutting each cube in half.

¼ teaspoon kosher salt

¼ teaspoon ground allspice

¼ teaspoon ground cinnamon

¼ teaspoon ground ginger

STREUSEL

1½ cups all-purpose flour

⅔ cup packed light brown sugar

1½ teaspoons ground cinnamon

¼ teaspoon kosher salt

¾ cup (1½ sticks) unsalted butter, straight from the fridge

4 ounces cream cheese, at room temperature, divided into 12 portions

Sugar-Sugar (see page 12), for sprinkling

Switch to a pastry blender and begin to cut in the butter with one hand while turning the bowl with the other. It's important not to aim for the same spot at the bottom of the bowl with each movement, but to actually slice through butter every time to maximize efficiency. Once most of the butter is incorporated, use your fingers to fully break down the butter until the streusel resembles wet sand. You can make the streusel up to 2 days in advance. Store in an airtight container in the refrigerator.

Preheat your oven to 400°F. Line a 12-cup muffin pan with paper liners, or generously grease the wells with butter or a natural nonstick cooking spray.

Use a spoon to fill each muffin cup about one-third full, then place 4 to 5 sweet potato chunks on top of each. Add one of the cream cheese portions and sprinkle generously with Sugar-Sugar. Use a small offset spatula or the back of a spoon to press down and spread the ingredients to the edge of the muffin liner. Scoop more muffin batter on top of each cup, until they are filled to just below the top of the liner. Spread again with a spatula or spoon. Distribute the streusel evenly over all of the muffins, making sure to press down on it to adhere.

Place the muffins in the oven and bake for 25 to 30 minutes, until a knife inserted into one of the middle muffins (near the perimeter, to bypass the cream cheese) comes out clean. Remove the pan from the oven and set it on a wire rack to cool.

Store leftover muffins in an airtight container in the refrigerator for up to 2 days.

How much '90s nostalgia can we fit into one weekend breakfast pastry? Time to find out.

My favorite stop at the mall as a preteen was not for daisy-covered T-shirts and chokers, as I'd have my friends believe, but for a sweet strawberry jam and cheese croissant from Vie de France. No amount of fashion approvals or slumber party invites could make me as content as slowly eating a flaky, buttery pastry encasing a tangy, creamy, fruity filling all by myself (while listening to Hanson on a Walkman, of course). It felt like a secret, a pastry that made sense only to me.

But I wasn't alone. When we asked our customers what pastries they most wanted to see in the display case at Sister Pie, an overwhelming number of them exclaimed, "Cheese danish!"

I've been determined to make something that evokes the same sensory experience, and this interpretation of a cinnamon bun is as close as I've gotten. You'll impress even the coolest middle-schoolers. ❤

LEMON POPPY BUNS

Makes 6 big buns

DOUGH

3 tablespoons unsalted butter

1 cup buttermilk

1 large egg, at room temperature

1 large egg yolk, at room temperature

½ cup granulated sugar

3½ cups all-purpose flour

1 tablespoon poppy seeds

2¼ teaspoons active dry yeast

1 teaspoon kosher salt

½ teaspoon packed grated lemon zest

FILLING

½ cup (1 stick) unsalted butter, at room temperature

8 ounces cream cheese, at room temperature

3 tablespoons granulated sugar

¼ teaspoon kosher salt

Want to mix and shape the buns the night before? That's actually what we do each weekend at the shop, so we might as well share our secret: Simply follow the steps through placing the assembled buns in the baking pan, then cover loosely with plastic wrap and place in the refrigerator. The next day, remove the pan from the fridge about 1 hour before you want to serve the buns. Place a shallow pan on the bottom of your (turned off) oven and fill it with boiling water from the tea kettle, then transfer the pan of buns to the oven and close the door. Set a timer for 45 minutes, then check to see if the buns are rising according to the proofing instructions. Remove the water pan and buns from the oven, and proceed with the baking instructions.

Make the dough: In a small saucepan over low heat, melt the butter. Add the buttermilk and warm until the mixture registers between 110° and 115°F on an instant-read thermometer. Meanwhile, place the egg and the yolk in the bowl of a stand mixer. Add the sugar and whisk by hand until combined. Stream in the warmed buttermilk mixture slowly, whisking as you go. Add ½ cup of the flour, the poppy seeds, yeast, salt, and lemon zest and whisk together, using the whisk to scrape down the sides if needed. Place the bowl onto the mixer fitted with the dough hook attachment and begin to mix on low speed.

CONTINUED

GLAZE

½ cup heavy cream,
at room temperature

1½ tablespoons coconut
oil, melted

3 tablespoons freshly
squeezed lemon juice

3 cups powdered sugar

1 tablespoon poppy seeds

¼ teaspoon kosher salt

Add the remaining 3 cups flour, ½ cup at a time, until it is completely absorbed. At this point, the dough will still feel sticky. Continue to knead on medium-low speed with the dough hook (or by hand on a lightly floured surface) until the dough is smooth and elastic, 5 to 7 minutes. Scrape the dough from the bowl and form into a ball. Lightly oil a large bowl. Place the dough in the oiled bowl and roll it around to coat it all over. Cover the bowl with a kitchen towel. Set aside to rise in a warm, draft-free place for 2 hours, until the dough has doubled in volume.

While the dough is rising, make the filling: In the bowl of a stand mixer, combine the butter, cream cheese, sugar, and salt. Fit the mixer with the paddle attachment and cream the mixture on medium speed until very smooth. Set aside, or store in the refrigerator, covered, for up to 2 days. Bring the filling to room temperature the day you plan to make the buns so it will be easy to spread.

Butter a 9 by 13-inch baking pan and dust it with flour, tilting the pan to evenly coat with flour. Dump out any excess flour.

Shape, proof, and bake the buns: Turn the risen dough out onto a generously floured surface. Deflate it with your hands and shape it into a rectangle. Using a rolling pin, gently roll the dough until it is about 14 inches long by 10 inches wide and ½ inch thick. Scrape all of the filling onto the center of the dough, and then use an offset spatula to evenly spread it across the entire surface, leaving just a ½-inch border around the perimeter. Starting at a short end, position your hands on the left and right sides, then roll the dough up as tightly and evenly as possible. You will likely need to move your hands to the center of the dough to catch it up with the sides. Gently squeeze the roll as you go to keep it tight and in place. Continue until you have reached the other end, then push the roll up so the seam side is facing down. You should end up with a short, fat log that is about 10 inches long. Using a sharp knife, mark the dough into 6 equal pieces, then slice.

Transfer the buns to the baking pan, spacing them at least ½ inch apart. Cover with a kitchen towel and set aside in a warm, draft-free place to proof for about 45 minutes.

PRINCESS T'S CHOCOLATE CHIP BUNS

Tianna, a pastry cook at Sister Pie, will often text me long after her shift has ended to share her latest menu ideas. One big winner was the chocolate chip–enriched edition of our Lemon Poppy Buns. To make these at home, omit the lemon zest and poppy seeds from the dough. Make the same filling, but when you go to roll up the buns, sprinkle them with ½ cup light brown sugar and ½ cup bittersweet chocolate chips. Just before baking, top the buns with 1½ tablespoons of Sugar-Sugar (see page 12) and a pinch of flaky sea salt. You won't make a glaze or icing for these, as they'll have developed a delightfully crunchy, salty-sweet exterior.

Preheat your oven to 375°F. Now sit down and read a book. I recommend *A Director Prepares*, by Anne Bogart.

The buns will rise to be about 1½ times larger than when you placed them in the pan. To test for readiness, press a finger onto the side of a bun—if it slowly but easily bounces back when you remove your finger, it's time to bake.

Remove the towel, transfer the pan to the oven, and bake for 30 to 35 minutes, until the buns are deeply golden in color. Remove the pan from the oven and set it on a cooling rack for at least 15 minutes.

While the buns are cooling, line a baking sheet with parchment paper and make the glaze: This is ostensibly the best part of a bun. Okay, it *is* the best part. In a medium bowl, combine the cream, coconut oil, lemon juice, powdered sugar, poppy seeds, and salt and whisk until very smooth. It should be pourable and not too thick.

Carefully remove the buns from the baking dish, one at a time, and set on the parchment-lined baking sheet. Pour a heaping ¼ cup of the glaze evenly over the top of each bun—it should easily drip down the sides. Place the baking sheet in a cool place to let the glaze fully set.

The buns are best eaten at room temperature within a few hours after baking, but you can also store them in an airtight container, or wrapped tightly in plastic (sorry, dear glaze), in the refrigerator for up to 2 days.

SOUTHEAST MICHIGAN'S FAVORITE HOLIDAY

Some celebrate Fat Tuesday to mark the beginning of Lent. We have Paczki Day instead. For us, it means working a 24-hour shift to mix, punch, fry, fill, and finish hundreds of Polish-style doughnuts, known plurally as paczki (say it with us: punch-KI) and singularly as paczek (punch-EK). For everybody else in our little part of the world, it means rising extra early (or skipping work entirely) to make a beeline for any paczki-making bakery, whether it's for the traditional prune- or custard-filled kind in Hamtramck or the nontraditional grapefruit- and hibiscus-filled paczki at Sister Pie. We usually sell out within the first hour, and then close for the rest of the day to recuperate.

This rich tradition was brought to America by Polish immigrants—we just made it bigger and into a consumer holiday. You can tell a classic paczki from other doughnuts by the lighter ring around the center of the outer circumference and the slightly collapsed center. In Poland, paczki are eaten on Fat Thursday, the day after Ash Wednesday, and Chicago, our friend to the west, enjoys paczki celebrations on Casimir Pulaski Day, which is on the first Monday in March, commemorating the Polish American revolutionary war general and honoring the Polish American community.

It's a pleasure-and-pain kind of event. For those making the paczki, it feels almost like an impossible challenge. Every year, Anji and I turn to each other and say in unison, "Never again." Those eating the paczki tend to consume too much, and the inevitable stomachache ensues. But as a community we choose to participate, year after year, in honor of a tradition that brings us stories and doughnuts. Only the strong survive!

Each year, we sell three riffs on the traditional paczki: one savory, one fruity, and one creamy. First up is this cream-filled, caffeinated beast. To make things easier on yourself, you can make the coffee pastry cream filling up to 2 days in advance and store in an airtight container in the refrigerator. ♥

MAPLE COFFEE CREAM PACZKI

Makes 10 paczki

COFFEE PASTRY CREAM

2 cups whole milk

¾ cup granulated sugar

¼ teaspoon kosher salt

¼ cup tapioca starch

1 tablespoon espresso powder

4 large egg yolks

2 tablespoons (¼ stick) unsalted butter, cut into cubes

1 teaspoon pure vanilla extract

DOUGH

1 cup buttermilk

2¼ teaspoons active dry yeast

¼ cup plus 1½ teaspoons granulated sugar

2½ cups all-purpose flour

1 large egg

2 large egg yolks

2 tablespoons espresso powder

1 teaspoon kosher salt

½ teaspoon pure vanilla extract

2 tablespoons (¼ stick) unsalted butter, melted and cooled

Canola oil, for frying

First, make the pastry cream: In a heavy-bottomed saucepan over medium-low heat, whisk 1½ cups of the milk, ½ cup of the sugar, and the salt. Slowly bring the mixture to a boil, continuing to stir occasionally to prevent the milk from scorching.

Meanwhile, in a medium bowl, whisk together the remaining ¼ cup sugar with the tapioca starch and espresso powder. Add the remaining ½ cup milk and the egg yolks. Whisk until smooth.

Once the milk comes to a boil, remove the pan from the heat. Add the milk mixture to the bowl with the egg yolk mixture, ¼ cup at a time, whisking constantly. Continue to do this until there is only about ½ cup left in the saucepan. Now pour all of the yolk-milk mixture back into the saucepan. Place the saucepan over medium-low heat and whisk constantly until the pastry cream has thickened. Remove from the heat and whisk in the butter and vanilla until smooth.

Transfer the pastry cream to a bowl and place a piece of plastic wrap directly on the surface to avoid a film developing while it cools. Transfer to the refrigerator to fully cool, or for up to 2 days.

Speaking of paczki, let's make that dough: Gently heat the buttermilk in a small saucepan over low heat until it registers between 110° and 115°F on an instant-read thermometer. Pour the warmed buttermilk into the bowl of a stand mixer. Add the yeast and whisk to dissolve. Add 1½ teaspoons of the sugar and ½ cup of the flour and mix until the ingredients are combined but still look a little chunky. Cover with plastic wrap and set aside to rest in a warm, draft-free place for 30 minutes, or until the starter is bubbly and has come alive.

CONTINUED

GLAZE

½ cup plus 2 tablespoons virgin refined coconut oil, melted

1½ cups powdered sugar

¾ cup maple syrup (Grade B if possible)

Espresso powder, for sprinkling tops

In a medium bowl, combine the egg and yolks, whisking until light and frothy, about 4 minutes. Whisk in the espresso powder, the remaining ¼ cup of sugar, and the salt and vanilla. Once the yeast starter is ready, stir in the melted butter and the egg mixture and whisk until just combined. Place the bowl on the stand mixer fitted with the dough hook and mix in the remaining 2 cups flour, ½ cup at a time, mixing on medium speed until a soft and sticky dough comes together, about 3 minutes. Continue to knead the dough with the hook for 7 minutes, or until very smooth. Grease a large bowl with oil or butter. Scrape the dough out of the mixer bowl into the greased bowl and cover with a kitchen towel. Set in a warm, draft-free place to rise for about 1 hour, until it has doubled in size.

Line two baking sheets with parchment paper.

Once the dough has doubled in size, turn it out onto a very generously floured surface. Dust the surface of the dough with flour, then gently deflate it until it is about ½ inch thick. Cut out the doughnuts with a 3½-inch round cutter or any other kind of cutter you like—feel free to get creative. Use a bench scraper to carefully transfer the doughnut rounds to the baking sheets, placing them 1½ inches apart. Gather the remaining dough and pat it out again and cut out another set of doughnuts. You should rework the dough only once. Cover the doughnuts with clean dish towels and set them in a warm, draft-free place to rise until doubled in size, about 30 minutes.

It's high time we started frying, so pour canola oil into a large Dutch oven or heavy-bottomed pot to a depth of 2 inches. Heat the oil to 380°F. While you're waiting, line a couple of wire racks with paper towels. Once the oil reaches the proper temperature, use a pair of heat-resistant tongs to carefully drop the paczki in, one at a time, cooking a maximum of three at a time. Cook the paczki until they turn deep golden brown on one side (about 3 minutes), then turn them and cook the other side until they reach the same degree of doneness (about 3 more minutes). Remove each paczek from the oil, letting any excess oil drain off into the Dutch oven before transferring to the wire rack. Before you fry the next three, bust open one paczek to check for doneness. Adjust the frying time for the next set accordingly and repeat until the paczki are all cooked.

To fill those paczki, insert a paring knife into the side of each paczek and jiggle it from side to side and up and down to create a pocket for the filling. Use a pastry bag fitted with a round tip or a small spoon to fill each paczek with about 3 tablespoons of the coffee cream.

Glaze those paczki: In a small mixing bowl, whisk together the coconut oil, powdered sugar, and maple syrup until very smooth. Remove the paper towels from the cooling racks and place them underneath the cooling racks to catch the extra glaze. Dip the top half of each filled paczek into the glaze, and then place on the wire racks and immediately sprinkle the espresso powder over them. Let the packzi rest for 10 minutes, or until the glaze is set, before serving. Paczki are best eaten fresh on the day they're made, but you could store them, refrigerated, in an airtight container or tightly wrapped in plastic for up to 2 days.

Our other sweet paczki offering is always fruity and representative of our love for the combination of floral and citrus flavors. You can make the curd filling up to 2 days in advance and store in an airtight container in the refrigerator. ♥

GRAPEFRUIT HIBISCUS PACZKI

Makes 10 paczki

GRAPEFRUIT HIBISCUS CURD

1⅓ cups granulated sugar

8 large egg yolks

3 tablespoons packed grated grapefruit zest

1 cup freshly squeezed grapefruit juice

⅓ cup dried hibiscus flowers, finely ground in a spice or coffee grinder

½ cup plus 2 tablespoons (1¼ sticks) unsalted butter, cut into ½-inch cubes

DOUGH

1 cup buttermilk

2¼ teaspoons active dry yeast

¼ cup granulated sugar plus 1½ teaspoons granulated sugar

2½ cups all-purpose flour

¼ cup dried hibiscus flowers, finely ground in a spice or coffee grinder

1 large egg

2 large egg yolks

1 teaspoon kosher salt

½ teaspoon pure vanilla extract

2 tablespoons (¼ stick) unsalted butter, melted and cooled

Canola oil, for frying

First, make the curd: In a heavy-bottomed saucepan over medium-low heat, combine the sugar, egg yolks, grapefruit zest and juice, and hibiscus. Whisk constantly until slightly thickened, which can take as long as 20 minutes, so I hope you're not in a rush. Remove from the heat and add the butter, a couple of cubes at a time, stirring after each addition to move along the melting process. Transfer the finished curd to a clean container and place a piece of plastic wrap directly on the surface to avoid a film developing while it cools. Transfer to the refrigerator to fully cool, or for up to 2 days.

Let's make that dough: Gently heat the buttermilk in a small saucepan over low heat until it registers between 110° and 115°F on an instant-read thermometer. Pour the warmed buttermilk into the bowl of a stand mixer. Add the yeast and whisk to dissolve. Add 1½ teaspoons of the sugar and ½ cup of the flour and mix until the ingredients are combined but still look a little chunky. Cover with plastic wrap and set aside to rest in a warm, draft-free place for 30 minutes, or until the starter is bubbly and has come alive.

In a medium bowl, combine the egg and yolks, whisking until light and frothy, about 4 minutes. Whisk in the remaining ¼ cup sugar and the salt and vanilla.

Once the yeast starter is ready, stir in the melted butter and the egg mixture and whisk until just combined. Place the bowl on the stand mixer fitted with the dough hook and mix in the remaining 2 cups flour, ½ cup at a time, mixing on medium speed until a soft and sticky dough comes together. Continue to knead with the dough hook for 7 minutes, or until very smooth.

CONTINUED

COATING

1 cup powdered sugar

2 tablespoons dried hibiscus flowers, finely ground in a spice or coffee grinder

Grease a large bowl with oil or butter. Scrape the dough out of the mixer bowl into the greased bowl and cover with a kitchen towel. Set in a warm, draft-free place to rise for about 1 hour, or until it has doubled in size.

Line a baking sheet with parchment paper.

Once the dough has doubled in size, turn it out onto a very generously floured surface. Dust the surface of the dough with flour, then gently deflate it until it is about ½ inch thick. Cut out the doughnuts with a 3½-inch round cutter or any other kind of cutter you feel like using—feel free to get creative. Use a bench scraper to carefully transfer the doughnut rounds to the baking sheet, placing them 1½ inches apart. Gather the remaining dough and pat it out again and cut out another set of doughnuts. You should rework the dough only once. Cover the doughnuts with a clean dish towel and set in a warm, draft-free place to rise until doubled in size, about 30 minutes.

It's high time we started frying, so pour canola oil into a large Dutch oven or heavy-bottomed pot to a depth of 2 inches. Heat the oil to 380°F. While you're waiting, line a wire rack with paper towels. Once the oil reaches the proper temperature, use a pair of heat-resistant tongs to carefully drop the paczki in the oil, one at a time, cooking a maximum of three at a time. Cook the paczki until they turn deep golden brown on one side (about 3 minutes), then turn them and cook the other side until they reach the same degree of doneness (about 3 more minutes). Remove each paczek from the oil, letting any excess oil drain off into the Dutch oven before transferring to the wire rack. Before you fry the next three, bust open one paczek to check for doneness. Adjust the frying time for the next set accordingly and repeat until the paczki are all cooked.

To fill those paczki, insert a paring knife into the side of each paczek and jiggle it from side to side and up and down to create a pocket for the filling. Use a pastry bag fitted with a round tip or a small spoon to fill each paczek with about 3 tablespoons of the curd.

Coat those paczki: Whisk the powdered sugar and hibiscus powder together in a medium bowl. Toss each paczek in the sugar topping, then transfer to the cooling rack or baking sheet.

Paczki are best eaten fresh on the day they're made, but you could store them, refrigerated, in an airtight container or tightly wrapped in plastic for up to 2 days.

Pieraczki is a word we made up to describe the fantastical hybrid made by combining pierogi and the famous Polish doughnut. Not everyone appreciates the sugar bombs that descend upon our area every Fat Tuesday, so this savory potato mash-up is for them.

Farmer's cheese (or farmer cheese) is pressed cottage cheese. If your local grocery doesn't stock it, substitute feta or drained ricotta. You can make the filling up to 2 days in advance and store it in an airtight container in the refrigerator. ♥

PIERACZKI (A PIEROGI-PACZKI HYBRID)
Makes 10 pieraczki

CHEESY POTATO FILLING

1½ pounds Yukon Gold potatoes, scrubbed and chopped into ½-inch chunks

1 tablespoon olive oil

1 to 2 large yellow onions, thinly sliced lengthwise (3 cups)

1 teaspoon light brown sugar

½ teaspoon kosher salt, plus more as needed

Splash of apple cider vinegar (optional)

4 ounces farmer's cheese

Freshly ground black pepper

DOUGH

1 cup buttermilk

2¼ teaspoons active dry yeast

¼ cup plus 1½ teaspoons granulated sugar

3½ cups all-purpose flour

1 large egg

3 large egg yolks

1 teaspoon kosher salt

2 tablespoons (¼ stick) unsalted butter, melted and cooled

Canola oil, for frying

Make the filling: Bring a large pot of salted water to a boil over high heat. Add the potatoes, decrease the heat to medium-low, and simmer until fork-tender. Drain, then transfer back to the pot. Use a potato masher or fork to mash the potatoes—they should be smooth, with the occasional chunk or two. What a delight. Reserve ⅔ cup mashed potato for the dough, and transfer the remainder to a mixing bowl.

Meanwhile, heat the olive oil in a large skillet over medium heat. Stir in the onions and brown sugar. Cook over medium-low heat, stirring often, until the onions begin to turn golden. After about 10 minutes, add the salt and continue to cook until the onions are deep brown and jammy. If the pan has lots of onion stuck to it, add a splash of apple cider vinegar and use your silicone spatula to scrape them up as the vinegar sizzles and releases what's stuck. Remove from the heat and set aside to cool for about 10 minutes. Add the onions to the mixing bowl with the potatoes. Add the farmer's cheese and mix until thoroughly combined. Taste and season with salt and pepper as needed.

Let's make that dough: In a small saucepan over low heat, gently heat the buttermilk until it registers between 110° and 115°F on an instant-read thermometer. Pour the warmed buttermilk into the bowl of a stand mixer. Add the yeast and whisk to dissolve. Add 1½ teaspoons of the sugar and ½ cup of the flour and mix until the ingredients are combined but still look a little chunky. Cover with plastic wrap and set aside to rest in a warm, draft-free place for 30 minutes, or until the starter is bubbly and alive.

CONTINUED

In a medium bowl, combine the egg and yolks. Whisk until light and frothy, about 4 minutes. Whisk in the remaining ¼ cup sugar and the salt.

Once the yeast starter is ready, stir in the melted butter, then the egg mixture and the reserved ⅔ cup mashed potatoes and whisk until just combined. Place the bowl on the stand mixer fitted with a dough hook and mix in the remaining 3 cups flour, ½ cup at a time, on medium speed until a soft and sticky dough comes together. Continue to knead with the dough hook for 7 minutes, or until very smooth.

Grease a large bowl with oil or butter. Scrape the dough out of the mixer bowl and into the greased bowl and cover with a kitchen towel. Set in a warm, draft-free place to rise for about 1 hour, until it has doubled in size.

Line two baking sheets with parchment paper.

Once the dough has doubled in size, turn it out onto a very generously floured surface. Dust the surface of the dough with flour, then gently deflate it until it is about ½ inch thick. Cut out the doughnuts with a 3½-inch round cutter or any other kind of cutter you like—feel free to get creative. Use a bench scraper to carefully transfer the doughnut rounds to the baking sheets, placing them 1½ inches apart. Gather the remaining dough and pat it out again, and cut out another set of doughnuts. You should rework the dough only once. Cover the baking sheets with clean dish towels and set in a warm, draft-free place to rise until doubled in size, about 30 minutes.

It's high time we started frying, so pour the canola oil into a large Dutch oven or heavy-bottomed pot to a depth of 2 inches. Heat the oil to 380°F. While you're waiting, line a couple of wire racks with paper towels. Once the oil reaches the proper temperature, use a pair of heat-resistant tongs to carefully drop the pieraczki in, one at a time, cooking a maximum of three at a time. Cook the pieraczki until they turn deep golden brown on one side (about 3 minutes), then turn them and cook the other side until they reach the same degree of doneness (about 3 more minutes). Remove each pieraczek from the oil, letting any excess oil drain off into the Dutch oven before transferring to the wire rack. Before you fry the next three, bust open one pieraczek to check for doneness. Adjust the frying time for the next set accordingly and repeat until the pieraczek are all cooked.

To fill those paczki, insert a paring knife into the side of each pieraczek and jiggle it from side to side and up and down to create a pocket for the filling. Use a pastry bag fitted with a round tip or a small spoon to fill each pieraczek with about 3 tablespoons of the onion-potato filling. Serve immediately while still warm. To rewarm, place them on a baking sheet in a 350°F oven for 5 to 10 minutes.

Pieraczki are best eaten fresh on the day they're made, but you could store them, refrigerated, in an airtight container or tightly wrapped in plastic for up to 2 days.

One Sunday we served savory waffles at the shop. We haven't done it since, but they were glorious, and here are they are. If you're really smart, you'll serve these with a medium-boiled egg on top. ♥

ROASTED ASPARAGUS, POTATO, AND CHIVE WAFFLES

Makes 4 to 6 waffles

ROASTED VEGETABLES

8 ounces asparagus, trimmed of woody ends and sliced into ¼-inch pieces

8 ounces Yukon Gold potatoes, scrubbed and diced into ½-inch pieces

2 tablespoons olive oil

½ teaspoon kosher salt

Freshly ground black pepper

BATTER

1¼ cups all-purpose flour

2 teaspoons baking powder

1 teaspoon baking soda

1 teaspoon kosher salt

¼ teaspoon freshly ground black pepper

1 teaspoon granulated sugar

¾ cup buttermilk

¾ cup sour cream

2 large eggs, at room temperature, separated

½ cup (1 stick) unsalted butter, melted and cooled, plus 1 to 2 tablespoons more for the waffle maker

4 ounces aged Cheddar cheese, grated, plus more for topping

¼ cup minced chives, plus more for topping

First, roast the vegetables: Preheat your oven to 450°F. In two separate bowls, toss the asparagus and the potatoes each with 1 tablespoon olive oil, ¼ teaspoon salt, and several grinds of black pepper. Arrange the asparagus and potatoes in a single layer on two baking sheets, and transfer to the oven. The asparagus will be done after about 10 minutes; you should be able to pierce it with a fork easily, but it should not be soft. Once you've set the asparagus down to cool, use a spatula to toss the potatoes on the baking sheet and return to the oven. They will be fork-tender and slightly golden brown on the edges when ready, after roasting for a total of 25 to 30 minutes. Remove from the oven and set aside to cool.

Once the vegetables have cooled, make the waffle batter: In a large bowl, whisk together the flour, baking powder, baking soda, salt, pepper, and sugar. In a medium bowl, whisk together the buttermilk, sour cream, egg yolks, and melted butter. Pour the buttermilk mixture over the dry mixture and use a silicone spatula to combine, mixing only until no dry spots remain. Once the vegetables have cooled, add them to the batter, along with the Cheddar and chives, and fold until combined.

Now's a pretty darn good time to fire up that waffle maker.

Using a stand mixer fitted with a whisk attachment or a hand mixer, whip the egg whites on the highest speed until soft peaks form. Use a silicone spatula to scrape half of the egg whites into the waffle batter, and gently fold in to incorporate, being careful not to deflate the egg whites. Repeat with the remaining egg whites. Your batter is ready!

CONTINUED

Use a pastry brush to grease the waffle maker lightly with butter. Scoop ¼ cup of the batter onto the center of each section of the iron. Close the waffle maker and—let's be honest . . . you know how yours works better than I do—cook until the waffle is deeply golden brown on top. Remove with tongs and transfer to a plate (or to a baking sheet if you're cooking for a crowd and you'd like to keep them warm in the oven). Repeat for the remainder of the batter.

Serve immediately, topped with plenty more grated Cheddar cheese and minced chives. If you don't intend to eat all of the waffles at once, when completely cool wrap them tightly in plastic or foil and store in the refrigerator for up to 2 days.

During the early days of Sister Pie, I'd spend Sunday afternoons at the shared commercial kitchen space, preparing pie and scone doughs for the week ahead. I was always trying to convince my close friends to stop by so they could hoist themselves up on a prep table and keep me company. The promise of cookies was my bargaining tactic, and it usually worked. On one of these Sundays, my friend Lizzy was nursing a serious hangover. What could I do to help? I had some scrap dough, a few potatoes, cheese, and eggs, and the first egg-on-top galette was born. It turned out to be just what the doctor ordered.

This is one of many egg-on-top galette combinations we've made over the years, but you should feel free as a bird to experiment with this basic formula. Try them with fresh ricotta, lots of black pepper, and red-skinned potatoes, or with whipped feta cheese topped with a pesto–white bean mix. The list of topping ideas goes on and on. ♥

EGG-ON-TOP SWEET POTATO AND CHEDDAR GALETTES

Makes eight 4-inch galettes

1 large sweet potato, sliced into thin rounds with a mandoline (or as thinly as you can hand-slice them)

1 tablespoon olive oil

¼ teaspoon kosher salt

Freshly ground black pepper

Buttermilk Buckwheat Galette Dough (page 39), rolled out into a 20-inch circle and laid flat on a parchment-lined baking sheet and refrigerated

8 ounces aged Cheddar cheese, grated

1 large egg, beaten

Flaky sea salt, for sprinkling

8 eggs, at room temperature

Dijon mustard, for serving

Place the sliced sweet potatoes in a large bowl, and toss evenly with the olive oil, salt, and pepper.

With the dough on the baking sheet, cut out 8 (4-inch) galette rounds and remove the dough scraps. Spread about 1 ounce Cheddar cheese on each round, leaving a border of about 1¼ inches. Arrange 4 to 6 slices of sweet potato on top of the cheese. Begin to seal the galettes by folding up a 1-inch section and pressing it down gently onto the sweet potatoes. Fold up the piece directly next to it, and place it down at an angle, so that it covers the corner of the dough you just laid down. Continue to do this until the entire circle is complete. Transfer the galettes to a baking sheet and place in your freezer for a 15-minute rest while you preheat the oven to 450°F.

Transfer the galettes to a parchment-lined baking sheet. Brush the tops and sides of the crusts with the beaten egg, and sprinkle with a few flakes of sea salt onto each. Place the baking sheet in the oven and bake for 20 to 25 minutes, until the crust is deeply golden brown and the potatoes look crispy around the edges.

CONTINUED

Remove the baking sheet from the oven and set on a cooling rack. Reduce the oven temperature to 375°F—it helps if you crack the door open.

Once the galettes have cooled for 5 minutes, use your fingers to gently press down on the potatoes, as they may have puffed up during the initial baking. Think of it as creating a little space for the egg. Crack an egg on top of each galette, then season with sea salt and pepper.

Return the baking sheet to the oven and bake for 12 to 15 minutes, or until the egg whites are opaque and set.

Remove the baking sheet from the oven and set on a wire rack to cool. Serve the galettes immediately, with a big dollop of Dijon mustard on the side.

sister salads

Seeing as my favorite foods are pie and salad (and ice cream), it didn't take long for the family meals we served for staff lunch to become a permanent fixture on the menu. Customers would peer over the counter at the gargantuan stainless steel bowl, normally reserved for pie dough, filled with arugula, roasted asparagus, chickpeas, and sunflower seeds, and ask, "Hey, can I get some of that?" To answer the demand, the Sister Salad was born. It changes nearly every single day and is our freshest reflection of what is currently growing in Michigan.

In this chapter, you'll find family-style Sister Salads for every season, from roasted roots in cooler months to bowls of simply dressed raw vegetables in warmer months. Feel free to experiment beyond what's written on these pages. These aren't fancy salads by any means—they're meant to be accessible and adaptable. To whip up a simple salad, keep these basic tenets in mind: A good salad contains two or three seasonal vegetables (crisp greens, roasted roots, raw radishes, for example), a bean or grain (white beans, buckwheat groats, barley, for example), tons of fresh herbs, something crunchy (nuts and seeds are good), and a homemade, chill dressing (one that packs a punch but doesn't overpower).

You'll find all your Sister Pie dressing needs met in this chapter. Each is simple and balanced and contains ingredients you can find year round. Looking to take these dressings to another level? Try adding a big handful of minced fresh herbs.

I've often joked that I'd vote "mustard for president." It's the ultimate condiment, appearing in all but one of the Sister Pie dressings. Here, we use whole-grain mustard for a texturally enhanced veggie-chomping experience. ♥

VOTE MUSTARD DRESSING

Makes 1 cup

1 shallot, finely minced

2 teaspoons whole-grain Dijon mustard

2 tablespoons freshly squeezed lemon juice

¼ teaspoon kosher salt

⅛ teaspoon freshly ground black pepper

½ cup extra-virgin olive oil

In a small bowl, whisk together the shallot, mustard, lemon juice, salt, and pepper. Slowly stream in the olive oil while whisking until smooth. Taste and adjust the seasoning. To store, transfer to a jar with a tight-fitting lid and refrigerate for up to 1 week.

If mustard were president, tahini would make a great VP. Tahini—a Middle Eastern staple made simply of ground sesame seeds—provides the ultimate in creamy, nutty indulgence. ♥

TAHINI POPPY DRESSING

Makes 1 cup

2 cloves garlic, minced with ¼ teaspoon kosher salt

1 tablespoon freshly squeezed lemon juice

¼ cup tahini

2 tablespoons hot water

2 tablespoons thick, plain yogurt

1 tablespoon mild honey

1 tablespoon Dijon mustard

½ teaspoon kosher salt

1 tablespoon poppy seeds

¼ cup plus 2 tablespoons extra-virgin olive oil

In a small bowl, whisk together the garlic, lemon juice, tahini, hot water, yogurt, honey, mustard, salt, and poppy seeds. Slowly stream in the olive oil, whisking until smooth. Taste and adjust the seasoning. To store, transfer to a jar with a tight-fitting lid and refrigerate for up to 1 week.

Inspired by the creaminess and familiarity of America's number-one dressing (ranch!), we wanted to create something that both coated the vegetables and provided richness without demanding all the attention. ♥

BUTTERMILK BLACK PEPPER DRESSING

Makes 1 cup

2 cloves garlic, finely minced with ¼ teaspoon kosher salt

½ cup buttermilk

⅔ cup thick, plain yogurt

1½ teaspoons apple cider vinegar

1 tablespoon extra-virgin olive oil

¼ teaspoon kosher salt

1 teaspoon freshly ground black pepper

In a small bowl, whisk together the garlic, buttermilk, yogurt, vinegar, olive oil, salt and pepper. Taste and adjust the seasoning. To store, transfer to a jar with a tight-fitting lid and refrigerate for up to 1 week.

The miso paste and chopped capers in this dressing provide the richness and umami to make a perfect accompaniment for crisp, raw vegetables. If you're out of lemons, substitute 2 teaspoons caper juice from the jar. ♥

CAPER MISO DRESSING

Makes 1 cup

1 tablespoon white miso paste (yellow in color, often labeled "sweet")

2 tablespoons hot water

2 cloves garlic, finely minced with ¼ teaspoon kosher salt

1 tablespoon Dijon mustard

1 tablespoon finely chopped capers

2 teaspoons freshly squeezed lemon juice

1 teaspoon mild honey

½ cup extra-virgin olive oil

Pinch of freshly ground black pepper

In a small bowl, whisk together the miso paste, hot water, garlic, mustard, capers, lemon juice, and honey. Slowly stream in the olive oil, whisking until smooth. Whisk in the pepper. Taste and adjust the seasoning. To store, transfer to a jar with a tight-fitting lid and refrigerate for up to 1 week.

What do celery, radishes, and parsley have in common? They're the kind of vegetables we grab to help build or complement flavor in other dishes. Rarely, though, do we utilize all of them at once, leading us to find a sad, shriveled pile of vegetables in the back of the crisper drawer. At Sister Pie, we have a very forward "use everything" approach, and you can usually see that reflected in the daily salad offering. This particular rendition is a catch-all for the aforementioned vegetables. Ten minutes of chopping and a quick salad dressing later, and you've got a light, crunchy, and resourceful dish.

If you just want to make this salad because it sounds good, go for it! Buy the ingredients specifically for that purpose. If you do happen to have leftovers from other recipes, use whatever you have and adjust the amount of dressing you mix in. ♥

CELERY, RADISH, PARSLEY, AND SUNFLOWER SEED SALAD

Makes 4 servings

1 head celery, stalks trimmed and sliced into ¼-inch pieces on the diagonal, leaves reserved

1 bunch (7 to 8) radishes, trimmed and sliced into ⅛-inch-thick half-moons

1 bunch parsley, leaves pulled from stems and coarsely chopped

¾ cup Caper Miso Dressing (page 229), plus more as needed

½ cup sunflower seeds, toasted (see page 35)

In a large serving dish, combine the celery, radishes, and parsley. Pour ¾ cup of the dressing on top and use a spoon to gently incorporate. Add more dressing if desired.

Top the salad with the sunflower seeds and reserved celery leaves. Serve immediately, with bread or crackers to sop up the juices. This salad is best eaten right after mixing, but it can also be assembled, except for the sunflower seeds, which should be added right before serving, and stored in the refrigerator in an airtight container for up to 2 days.

My grandmother, whom we affectionately call Mimi (pronounced MIH-mee), would love to tell you about the time that I used salt instead of sugar in the first cookie recipe I developed, at age eight or so. What she might not realize, however, is that my affinity for salt came directly from her. One of my favorite summertime snacks as a kid was Mimi's cucumbers. She would peel and slice the cucumbers about ¼ inch thick and arrange them on a china plate. Then she'd just pour the salt on top. This salad goes out to Mimi. ♥

SALTY CUKES AND CRISPY BULGUR SALAD

Makes 4 servings

1½ cups peeled, sliced cucumbers (any variety, seeded or not), sliced into ½-inch-thick half-moons

1¼ teaspoons kosher salt

1 head broccoli, cut into small florets

¼ cup plus 1 tablespoon extra-virgin olive oil

½ teaspoon freshly ground black pepper

¼ cup bulgur wheat

5 ounces butter lettuce, ripped into bite-size pieces

½ cup crumbled feta cheese

¼ cup minced fresh mint leaves

½ cup Buttermilk Black Pepper Dressing (page 229)

¼ teaspoon ground sumac

In a colander, toss the cucumbers with 1 teaspoon of the salt. Let stand for 30 minutes for the cucumbers to release some of their moisture.

While the cucumbers are standing, prepare the broccoli: Preheat your oven to 425°F. Place the broccoli on a baking sheet and toss with 1 tablespoon of the olive oil, ¼ teaspoon of the salt, and the pepper. Transfer the baking sheet to the oven and roast for 30 to 35 minutes, or until the broccoli is fork-tender and caramelized.

Next, cook and fry the bulgur: In a medium saucepan, bring 1 cup water to a boil. Add the bulgur and bring to a boil. Decrease the heat to a simmer, cover, and cook until tender, about 10 minutes. Drain in a colander to remove the excess liquid, and transfer to a plate. Spread the bulgur out in an even layer and pat dry with a paper towel. In a small sauté pan, heat the remaining ¼ cup olive oil until shimmering. Add the cooked bulgur and cook over medium heat until golden brown and crispy, 5 to 6 minutes, stirring the bulgur occasionally to avoid clumping. Remove the bulgur from the oil and drain on a paper towel–lined plate. Season with a pinch of salt.

To serve, place the butter lettuce in a large serving bowl and top with the cucumbers, roasted broccoli, crispy bulgur, feta, mint, and the dressing and use a spoon to gently incorporate. Finish with a sprinkling of sumac.

This salad is best eaten right after mixing, but it can also be assembled, except for the butter lettuce, which should be mixed in right before serving, and stored in the refrigerator in an airtight container for up to 2 days.

At the shop, we go a little crazy, in a good way, roasting summer vegetables until they're practically falling apart, ratatouille-style. Mixed with a grain and some kinda green, it's the light lunch everyone is craving come July and August. This hearty summer salad can be served the day after it is made, cold from the cooler at the lake, or freshly mixed at home, warm from the heat of the lentils and roasted vegetables.

You could easily modify this recipe to include other summertime vegetables . . . such as broccoli. ♥

EGGPLANT, SUMMER SQUASH, AND LENTIL SALAD

Makes 4 servings

1 pound eggplant, cut into 1-inch chunks

2 pounds summer squash (zucchini, yellow, pattypan), cut into 1-inch chunks

2 tablespoons extra-virgin olive oil

1 teaspoon plus a pinch of kosher salt

1 teaspoon freshly ground black pepper

1 cup black lentils, rinsed and sorted through

½ cup plus 1 tablespoon thinly sliced chives

¾ cup Caper Miso Dressing (page 229), plus more as needed

First, roast the vegetables: Preheat your oven to 425°F. Place the eggplant and squash on two separate baking sheets and toss evenly with the olive oil, 1 teaspoon salt, and the pepper. Transfer the baking sheets to the oven and roast for 30 to 40 minutes, or until the eggplant and squash are fork-tender and caramelized. Set the pans on wire racks to cool.

Meanwhile, cook the lentils: In a medium saucepan, bring 3 cups water and a generous pinch of salt to a rolling boil. Add the lentils, decrease the heat to a simmer, and cook until tender, 20 to 25 minutes. Drain off any excess liquid. Transfer the lentils to a salad serving bowl and toss with ½ cup of the chives.

Add the roasted eggplant and squash to the bowl with the lentils. Pour ¾ cup of the dressing over the salad and use a spoon to gently incorporate. Taste and adjust the seasoning, adding more dressing if desired. Top with the remaining 1 tablespoon chives.

This salad is best eaten right after mixing, but it can also be assembled and stored in the refrigerator in an airtight container for up to 2 days.

Toward the beginning of fall, we are still joyfully receiving a wide variety of vegetables from the vitamin C– and fiber-packed brassica family, and cauliflower is a clear favorite. When roasting, the cauliflower perfumes the entire bakery with a defiantly non-pie scent. The addition of barley, golden raisins, and pistachios makes this salad très SP. ♥

TWO-WAY CAULIFLOWER AND BARLEY SALAD

Makes 4 servings

1 head cauliflower, cut into florets

1 tablespoon olive oil

¼ teaspoon plus a pinch of kosher salt

½ teaspoon freshly ground black pepper

1 cup hulled barley

½ cup golden raisins, soaked briefly in 1 cup warm water and drained

¾ cup Tahini Poppy Dressing (page 228), plus more as needed

½ cup roasted, salted pistachios, coarsely chopped

First, prepare the cauliflower: Preheat your oven to 400°F. Place half of the cauliflower florets on a baking sheet and toss with the olive oil, ¼ teaspoon of the salt, and the pepper. Transfer to the oven and bake for 30 to 35 minutes, until the cauliflower is fork-tender and caramelized.

Slice the remaining cauliflower florets into ¼-inch-thick cross-sections.

Cook the barley: In a medium saucepan over medium-high heat, combine the barley, 3 cups water, and a big pinch of salt. Bring to a boil. Decrease the heat to low, cover, and continue to cook until the barley is tender but retains an al dente chew, 40 to 45 minutes. Drain any excess water, transfer to a large bowl, and let cool.

In a large serving bowl, combine the roasted and raw cauliflower, barley, and raisins. Pour ¾ cup of the dressing over the salad and use a spoon to gently incorporate. Taste and adjust the seasoning, adding more dressing if desired. Top the salad with the pistachios.

This salad is best eaten right after mixing, but it can also be assembled, except for the pistachios, which should be added right before serving, and stored in the refrigerator in an airtight container for up to 2 days.

This is exactly the kind of warm salad bowl I want to come home to during a harsh, icy winter: tender and wholesome buckwheat groats, velvety and sweet roasted roots, and tangy caramelized leeks, all tossed with fresh, bitter arugula. Not much more to say, is there? ♥

BUCKWHEAT, CARROT, PARSNIP, AND LEEK SALAD

Makes 4 servings

1 pound carrots, peeled and cut into 1-inch-long by ½-inch-wide pieces on the diagonal

1 pound parsnips, peeled and cut into 1-inch-long by ½-inch-wide pieces on the diagonal

3 tablespoons olive oil

¾ teaspoon kosher salt

¾ teaspoon freshly ground black pepper

2 leeks, trimmed and julienned

1 tablespoon balsamic vinegar

1 cup buckwheat groats, toasted (see page 35)

4 cups loosely packed arugula

¾ cup Tahini Poppy Dressing (page 228), plus more as needed

½ cup pepitas, toasted (see page 35)

Preheat your oven to 400°F. Place the carrots and parsnips on a baking sheet and toss with 2 tablespoons of the olive oil, ½ teaspoon of the salt, and ½ teaspoon of the pepper. Transfer to the oven and roast for 45 to 50 minutes, until the carrots and parsnips are fork-tender. Set on a cooling rack.

Fill a large bowl with cold water. Slosh the leeks around in the water to remove the dirt. Using a spider, transfer the leeks to a clean kitchen towel and pat them dry. Place the leeks on a baking sheet and toss with the remaining 1 tablespoon olive oil, ¼ teaspoon salt, ¼ teaspoon pepper, and the vinegar. Transfer to the oven and roast for 25 to 30 minutes, until the leeks are caramelized. Set on a cooling rack.

To cook the buckwheat groats, in a medium saucepan over high heat, bring 2 cups water to a boil. Add the toasted buckwheat groats and return to a full boil. Decrease the heat to medium-low, cover, and simmer until all of the water has been absorbed, about 10 minutes. Transfer to a bowl and set aside until fully cool.

Place the arugula in a large serving bowl, then add the carrots, parsnips, leeks, and buckwheat. Pour ¾ cup of the dressing over the salad and use a spoon to gently incorporate. Taste and adjust the seasoning, adding more dressing if desired. Top with the pepitas and serve.

This salad is best eaten right after mixing, but it can also be assembled, except for the arugula and pepitas, which should be added right before serving, and stored in the refrigerator in an airtight container for up to 2 days.

EPILOGUE

My understanding of what sisterhood means has expanded over the course of my lifetime and will, I trust, continue to transform. It began when my sister Sarah was born and I learned to share. It continued as I made childhood friends, gleaning something new from each one as I discovered how to listen. It matures still in my role as a boss, working to develop inclusive values and practices. As a community member, I've grown to comprehend that I can and should question what has been made to seem normal. This path has not been perfect—I've made a million mistakes, burned bridges, and thought I knew it all before I knew enough.

I had never considered opening a business until I considered opening one in Detroit. Every moment spent in this city surrounds me with kind, resilient people who collectively care for the greater good of our home. Detroit is too often advertised to outsiders as a blank slate, a wonderland where creative types can roam freely. The reality is that people have been making it work for a long time in Detroit, thriving against serious odds and protecting each other. My own familial ties to the region, coupled with this understanding, gave me the confidence I needed to succeed here.

I happen to come from a family of family businesses. My grandfather started a plywood company in Detroit in 1967, and my father still runs it today. As times have changed, the meaning of family has changed, expanded, and become more complex and more interesting. Family is not only loyalty to your kin. By its new definition, a family is a social unit of people who relate to each other. The ties that bind families together are greater than blood. Sister Pie is a family business.

It is our duty in this world to evolve, to always ask questions, and to push constantly against a system that values some lives more than others. As a young, white woman running a business in Detroit, there's no denying my privilege. Yet as a business owner, I'm working to resist the patriarchal and capitalist norms that often define our work, our culture, and our world. I am surprised at how often the one I'm up against is me.

Thank you for joining me on this adventure. If you have questions, ideas for pie, tips to share, or you'd just like to say hi, come by the shop (8066 Kercheval, Detroit) or email me (lisa@sisterpie.com). The door and inbox are always open.

ACKNOWLEDGMENTS

Thank you:

To Lorena Jones, Ashley Lima, Kristin Casemore, Allison Renzulli, Serena Sigona, and everyone else at Ten Speed Press for the opportunity to share our pies with the world. This book is a beautiful collaboration.

To Emily Berger-Crawford, this book's photographer and my newfound friend: Your commitment to and vision for this project exceeded my wildest dreams. You make us look so good.

To Anji Reynolds Barto: You are a powerhouse of creativity, hustle, creeping skills, and kindness. I treasure our "complicated" friendship. Thanks for the dance duos, tolerating my chronic absentmindedness, and letting me leave for a month to write this thing.

To the shop parents, Mother Pie (Diane) and Father Ply (Kurt): I cannot contain my gratitude for you. Amid mistakes, triumphs, and all those times in my twenties when I asked you for money, you've continued to support my sassy, headstrong, weirdo self. Everything you did led me to here. I am eternally and profoundly thankful.

To the original Sister Pie, Sarah, my sibling and companion for life: I love you to "dog-heaven" and back.

To the rest of the Sister Pie staff, past and present: Thank you, Ashley Addrow-Pierson, Shameka Amos, Amy Anderson, Bridget Bailey, Shontasia Bass, Amber Beasley, Tianna Bogan, Brittney Bowen, Kara Bruhns, Anthea Calhoun-Bey, Shavonta Carson, Camille Chippewa, Reed Clancy, Josephine Corrado, Tyetonia Currie, Danielle Daguio, China Davis, Shanel DeWalt, Kristen Ellis, Amy Ervin, Dominica Estes, Lauren Glapa, Jessica Grabbe, Kamaria Gray, Morgan Hutson, MyThy Huynh, Avida Johnson, Beverly Johnson, Taylor Karabach, Casey Kempton, Maggie McGuire, Bri Meilbeck, Hannah Miller, Gabrielle Moses, Colin Packard, Jane Pastor, Zach Poley, Nicole Ponton, Maddy Rager, Maisie Rodriguez, Troi Rogers, Leanne Roznowski, Steve St. James, Erin Shawgo, Erin Sheehan, Starshay Tarleton, Molly Trahan, and Stephanie Vella.

To literary agent Kari Stuart: I'd be lost without your literary savvy and words of encouragement.

To Maddie LaKind: You've got the kind of swag no one can touch. Thanks for hammering out every single detail of this project with me, and for all the stomach openers in between, my dear friend.

To Hilary Fann, professional *and* home baker extraordinaire: There's no one I'd rather eat smoked whitefish dip with while watching a pure Michigan sunset. Thanks for traveling down holiday road once again, and working around the clock to tweak each tablespoon.

To the rest of my at-home recipe testing crew, Mike Behm, Tim Mazurek, Colin Packard, and Fiona Ruddy: Your tough love was always just right. Thank you for putting in a heck-ton of work on this and for always catching my typos.

To Meagan Elliott, Sister Pie's very own calligrapher and my ever-supportive sweet friend.

To a whole host of folks who have, in big and small ways, supported and shaped me, this bakery, and this book: Katie Asadi, Ryan Barto, Jeni Britton-Bauer, Bianca Colbath, Jess Daniel, Devita Davison, Jena Derman, Jamie Dessecker, Emily Elsen, Melissa Elsen, Emily Harpe, Ryan Hatch, Ben Houston, Helen Jo, Emilia Juocys, Vittoria Katanski, Anne LaTarte, Courtney McBroom, Matt McKenna, Jill Meyer, Ryan O'Byrne, Pam and Mark Reynolds, Nancy Schott, Irene "Mimi" Skarjune, Dustin Smith, Christina Tosi, and so many more.

INDEX